Ωmega Desktop, Inc.

Ω

Betty L. Boyce, M.A.
Business Education Consultant
Santa Maria, California

Mary S. Auvil, M.A.
Ohlone College, Fremont, California
Cabrillo College, Aptos, California

Patricia D. Whitman, Ed. D.
Business Education Consultant
Buena Park, California

A DESKTOP PUBLISHING SIMULATION

DF21AB
PUBLISHED BY
SOUTH-WESTERN PUBLISHING CO.
CINCINNATI, OH   DALLAS, TX   LIVERMORE, CA

Credits:
Acquisitions Editor: *Robert First*
Developmental Editor: *Diana Trabel*
Associate Editor: *Anne Noschang*
Editorial Associate: *Casey D. Doyle*
Production Artist: *Sophia Renieris*

Copyright ©1991

by SOUTH-WESTERN PUBLISHING CO.
Cincinnati, Ohio

ALL RIGHTS RESERVED

The text of this publication, or any part thereof, may not be reproduced or transmitted in any form or by any means, electronic or mechanical, including photocopying, recording, storage in an information retrieval system, or otherwise, without the prior written permission of the publisher.

ISBN: 0–538–60535–9

1 2 3 4 5 6 7 8 9 DH 8 7 6 5 4 3 2 1 0

Printed in the United States of America

PREFACE

Omega Desktop, Inc.: A Desktop Publishing Simulation is a generic text-workbook for beginning courses that introduce desktop publishing. This text-workbook assumes that you have **no prior experience** with desktop publishing software.

The text-workbook consists of ten chapters, each containing desktop publishing and editing activities. Moving from simple to complex, the goals of the text-workbook are designed to help you

- gain an understanding of desktop publishing concepts;
- learn to use desktop publishing software to publish a variety of documents;
- develop the ability to edit for more effective communication.

You are to save the assignments that you complete for your own publishing handbook. Your completed publishing handbook can be used as a portfolio to show others your expertise with desktop publishing software and your editing skill.

In **Chapter 1—Touring Your Software**, you

- start the computer and load the desktop publishing software;
- identify parts of the working screen, menus, and dialog boxes;
- edit to make text more specific;
- use selected proofreaders' marks;
- use desktop publishing terms correctly.

In **Chapter 2—Your First Desktop Publication**, you

- select page orientation and set margins;
- import and place text and graphics;
- save and print the combined text/graphic file;
- edit text by removing clichés and review how to proofread more effectively.

In **Chapter 3—Working with Text and Graphics**, you

- use thumbnail sketches to plan a page layout;
- use rulers to guide the placement of text and graphics;
- set margins and place text and graphics according to the layout;
- break text into blocks and insert a graphic into the text;
- make editorial changes in the text within the DTP software;
- edit copy to eliminate redundancies.

In **Chapter 4—Comparing Pasteup Techniques**, you

- compare manual and computerized pasteup;
- combine manual and computerized pasteup to create originals for photocopying;

- enter text directly in the DTP software;
- copy blocks of text;
- edit to eliminate wordiness.

In **Chapter 5—Working with Typefaces**, you
- learn to recognize common serif and sans serif typefaces;
- print sample pages using different typefaces, styles, sizes, and leading;
- select and specify type for appearance and readability;
- proofread for and correct punctuation errors.

In **Chapter 6—Communicating Through Page Layout**, you
- use a page grid to organize page layout;
- learn to recognize symmetrical and asymmetrical layouts;
- use variety and contrast in page design;
- use visual elements to communicate information;
- edit for grammatical errors.

In **Chapter 7—Using Graphics in Desktop Publishing**, you
- use DTP graphic tools to enhance layout;
- select and arrange graphics to support the text;
- learn to recognize different types of graphic files;
- write effective opening sentences and paragraphs.

In **Chapter 8—Experimenting with Page Layout**, you
- use large initial caps and drop caps;
- change text alignment;
- create headers and footers;
- use pull quotes and sidebars to set off text;
- use runaround text to set off a picture;
- adjust the layout and text for copyfitting;
- edit to delete needless prefaces and modifiers.

In **Chapter 9—Developing Products for Omega Desktop, Inc.**, you
- learn to ask the right questions when planning a publication;
- use special features of your DTP software to prepare makeovers, comprehensives, and mechanicals;
- create a variety of desktop-published products on your own;
- edit to vary sentence structure and length;
- apply basic word division rules;
- combine related thoughts and use short sentences for emphasis.

In **Chapter 10—Creating a Publishing Handbook**, you
- design and publish a cover for your handbook;
- create a title page;
- organize and publish a table of contents;
- edit for good organization.

A wide variety of desktop publishing software can be utilized to complete the assignments. However, the software you are using may not be capable of all the operations described. If not, plan to expand your skill with manual pasteup techniques by utilizing the printouts of the graphic files located in Appendix B. Additionally, you may discover that some of the features listed in each chapter's Software Check are not available with the software you are using. If this is the case, your teacher or an advanced student should discuss the limitations of your software with you. Although your software may have limitations, additional capabilities are available with other software. Keeping this in mind will help you transfer what you learn to more sophisticated software that you might use in the future.

Template disks, in $5^1/_4$-inch and $3^1/_2$-inch sizes, are available to support the following DTP software:
- Springboard Publisher™[1] for Apple® IIe, Apple IIc, Apple IIGS®[2]
- PFS:® First Publisher[3] for IBM®[4], Tandy®[5], and other IBM-compatible machines
- PageMaker® 3.0[6] for Macintosh®[7], IBM, Tandy, and other IBM-compatible machines

The template disks contain all the text and graphic files required for the activities. The files will enable you to experience updating, formatting, and integrating text and graphics without having to take the time to key the text or create original graphics.

---

[1]Springboard Publisher is a trademark of Springboard Software, Inc.

[2]Apple and IIGS are registered trademarks of Apple Computer, Inc.

[3]PFS:First Publisher is a registered trademark of Software Publishing Company.

[4]IBM is a registered trademark of International Business Machines Corporation.

[5]Tandy is a registered trademark of Tandy Corporation.

[6]PageMaker is a registered trademark of Aldus Corporation.

[7]Macintosh is a registered trademark of McIntosh Laboratory, Inc., and is used by Apple Computer, Inc., with its express permission.

CONTENTS

PREFACE   *iii*

INTRODUCTION   1

    Omega Desktop, Inc.—About the Company   1
    Features of This Book   1

1   TOURING YOUR SOFTWARE   3

    Chapter Objectives   3
    Introduction   4
    Software Check   7
    Fact Sheet: Desktop Publishing Software   9
    At the Editor's Desk   9
    You, the Editor!   11
    Exploring Desktop Publishing   13
    Vocabulary Review   15
    Treasure Hunt   16
    Work Assignment Log   16

2   YOUR FIRST DESKTOP PUBLICATION   17

    Chapter Objectives   17
    Introduction   18
    Software Check   21
    Fact Sheet: Importing Text and Graphics   23
    At the Editor's Desk   23
    You, the Editor!   25
    Exploring Desktop Publishing   29
    Vocabulary Review   33
    Treasure Hunt   34
    Work Assignment Log   34

3   WORKING WITH TEXT AND GRAPHICS   35

    Chapter Objectives   35
    Introduction   36
    Software Check   39
    Fact Sheet: Layout Tools   41

At the Editor's Desk   41
You, the Editor!   43
Exploring Desktop Publishing   49
Vocabulary Review   53
Treasure Hunt   54
Work Assignment Log   54

4 COMPARING PASTEUP TECHNIQUES   55

Chapter Objectives   55
Introduction   56
Software Check   59
Fact Sheet: Manual Pasteup Techniques   61
At the Editor's Desk   61
You, the Editor!   65
Exploring Desktop Publishing   69
Vocabulary Review   73
Treasure Hunt   74
Work Assignment Log   74

5 WORKING WITH TYPEFACES   75

Chapter Objectives   75
Introduction   76
Software Check   79
Fact Sheet: Information About Typefaces   81
At the Editor's Desk   82
You, the Editor!   83
Exploring Desktop Publishing   87
Vocabulary Review   93
Treasure Hunt   94
Work Assignment Log   94

6 COMMUNICATING THROUGH PAGE LAYOUT   95

Chapter Objectives   95
Introduction   96
Software Check   99
Fact Sheet: Page Layout Considerations   101
At the Editor's Desk   101
You, the Editor!   105

Exploring Desktop Publishing   109
Vocabulary Review   115
Treasure Hunt   116
Work Assignment Log   116

7 USING GRAPHICS IN DESKTOP PUBLISHING   117

Chapter Objectives   117
Introduction   118
Software Check   121
Fact Sheet: Using Graphic Images   123
At the Editor's Desk   123
You, the Editor!   127
Exploring Desktop Publishing   131
Vocabulary Review   135
Treasure Hunt   136
Work Assignment Log   136

8 EXPERIMENTING WITH PAGE LAYOUT   137

Chapter Objectives   137
Introduction   138
Software Check   141
Fact Sheet: Special Effects in Desktop Publishing   143
At the Editor's Desk   143
You, the Editor!   147
Exploring Desktop Publishing   149
Vocabulary Review   151
Treasure Hunt   152
Work Assignment Log   152

9 DEVELOPING PRODUCTS FOR OMEGA DESKTOP, INC.   153

Chapter Objectives   153
Introduction   154
Software Check   157
Fact Sheet: Desktop Publishing Software Features   159
At the Editor's Desk   160

You, the Editor! 163
Exploring Desktop Publishing 165
Vocabulary Review 173
Treasure Hunt 174
Work Assignment Log 174

10 CREATING A PUBLISHING HANDBOOK 175

Chapter Objectives 175
Introduction 176
Software Check 179
Fact Sheet: Completing
    the Publication Process 181
At the Editor's Desk 181
You, the Editor! 183
Exploring Desktop Publishing 189
Vocabulary Review 191
Treasure Hunt 192
Work Assignment Log 192

APPENDIX A 193

Proofreaders' Marks 195
Clichés 197
Redundant Phrases 199
Frequently Misspelled Business Words 201
Making Text More Concise by
    Eliminating Unnecessary Words and Phrases 203
Punctuation Guidelines 205
State Abbreviations 209

APPENDIX B 211

GLOSSARY 231

INDEX 241

INTRODUCTION

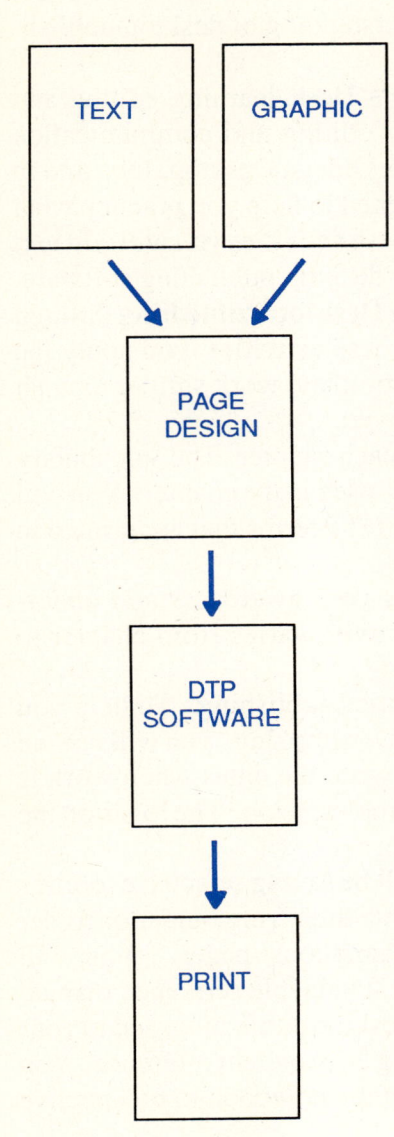

Omega Desktop, Inc.—About the Company

The owners of Omega Desktop, Inc., Aiko and Andy Koyama, have recently expanded their business. Today Omega Desktop, Inc., offers a wide variety of services. In the past, the services ranged from simple photocopying jobs to complex phototypesetting and pasteup jobs. With the expansion of the business, Aiko and Andy purchased several computers that have been made available for customers to rent. Customers can create their own newsletters and flyers. They can design their own business cards, letterhead, forms, and advertisements.

Desktop publishing (DTP) and graphics software are in demand. Omega customers frequently bring disks that contain word processing documents. When word processing files are brought into a desktop publishing program, the text can be formatted and graphics added. The Koyamas also have laser printers. When text and graphics are combined with a desktop publishing program and laser-printed, the resulting document looks professionally prepared. Customers like this professional appearance.

The desktop publishing software saves time making professional-looking pages. Before this software was available, the job of creating illustrations and combining them with text in page layouts was done by hand. When even minor changes were necessary, many hours of expensive hand work were usually required to adjust the page layouts. Today changes can be made easily by using desktop publishing. In a few minutes the Omega staff can produce a proof or sample print to show customers how their publications will look. Variations and revisions can be generated quickly with the DTP software. It's no wonder this new service is bringing more customers into the shop.

With the expansion, more employees are needed. You applied for a position and have just been hired at Omega Desktop, Inc. You are excited to learn about desktop publishing and the variety of activities performed in a modern photocopy shop.

Features of This Book

This book has several features in each chapter. A brief description of each follows.

The **Chapter Objectives** provide an overview of what you will be able to do when you finish a chapter. The **Introduction** gives you an overview of the chapter focus. It is a brief story about what you will be doing.

Each chapter contains a **Software Check** that will teach you about the software you are using. The Software Check will help expand your understanding of DTP concepts. Understanding concepts is important.

By understanding concepts, most people can learn new programs quickly.

The **Fact Sheet** gives you background information. Fact Sheet information also helps to build your understanding of desktop publishing concepts.

You will spend time **At the Editor's Desk** learning editing and communication skills. Sharpening your editing and communication skills is important to your success, both at Omega Desktop, Inc., and in the real world. **You, the Editor!** is designed to help you practice what you learn from At the Editor's Desk. In these activities you will edit text for the documents that you produce with desktop publishing software.

In each chapter you will be **Exploring Desktop Publishing** through a series of hands-on DTP activities. In these activities, you apply the concepts you learn in the chapter. You complete work similar to what you might do if you were actually employed.

A **Vocabulary Review** is included in each chapter. The Vocabulary Review will help you remember new terms used in the chapter. You will also find that each chapter contains many DTP terms that are printed in bold.

The **Treasure Hunt** further expands your awareness and understanding of desktop publishing. This activity varies from chapter to chapter and is sure to be an adventure.

Meeting deadlines is an everyday part of publishing. To help you keep track of your assignments at Omega Desktop, Inc., you will use the **Work Assignment Log**. Here you will write the dates when work is assigned, when it is due, and when you complete a job. The log is on the last page of each chapter.

As you complete assignments, you will be saving selected exercises for a publishing handbook. Plan to obtain a three-ring binder or folder with pockets to hold your publishing handbook pages. You will discover that your handbook will become a valuable reference manual during this course. As you continue with desktop publishing, add to your handbook. In this way, you will be creating an excellent reference. You can show the samples of work you save in the notebook to prospective employers and clients.

You might be interested to know that this book was produced using desktop publishing software. The authors hope you enjoy learning about desktop publishing as much as they enjoyed developing this book.

CHAPTER 1
TOURING YOUR SOFTWARE

Ω

CHAPTER OBJECTIVES

When you have completed this chapter, you will be able to:

✓ Start the computer and load the desktop publishing software.
✓ Identify parts of the working screen, menus, and dialog boxes.
✓ Edit text to make it more specific.
✓ Use selected proofreaders' marks in editing copy.
✓ Define selected desktop publishing terms.

INTRODUCTION

You and Stan Decatur are new part-time employees at Omega Desktop, Inc., a copy center. You will be working at the Omega shop in Santa Rosa, California. The owners, Aiko and Andy Koyama, entered the fast-growing photocopy business three years ago, shortly after coming to Santa Rosa. After two years, they expanded what was then known as Omega Copies, Inc. They added a do-it-yourself service. They purchased microcomputers and a variety of software, including desktop publishing software. For the first time, their customers could rent time on the computers to create their own documents. To handle the do-it-yourself customers, the Koyamas expanded their staff. They hired a graphic artist and an editor who are familiar with computers.

Do-it-yourself services, especially desktop publishing, have become popular. Since many customers use this service, Aiko and Andy changed the name of their business to Omega Desktop, Inc. To help with the increased number of customers, they hired you and Stan.

You are excited to be working at Omega Desktop, Inc. Now you will be able to work with computers using desktop publishing software. You and Stan both know how to use word processing programs. However, neither of you have much experience with graphics and desktop publishing software. Andy Koyama explains that in desktop publishing, pictures, or graphics, are as important as the words, or text.

"You will need to learn a little about desktop publishing and graphics programs," Andy says. He explains that you will be learning new vocabulary so you can talk to customers about the programs. Soon you will be combining text and graphic files to create all kinds of publications for the shop. You will also be creating publications and other documents for customers who do not have time to do it themselves. As you become familiar with the equipment and software, you will be expected to help customers who rent equipment to do their own work.

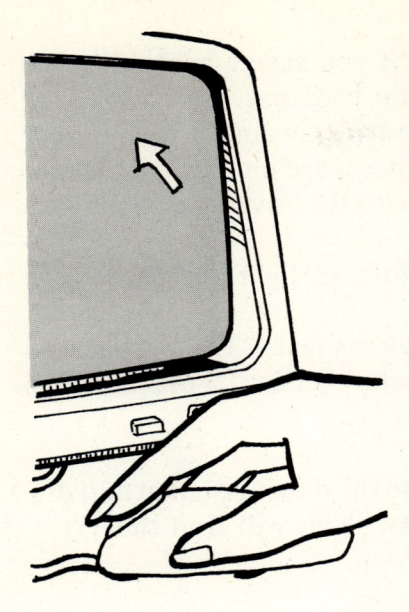

Many of your assignments will involve editing materials that you will publish. Andy asks you to save the worksheets that you complete for your assignments. Put them in a notebook to create a publishing handbook. You will find that your handbook will become a good reference for you both at Omega Desktop, Inc., and for your personal use.

Andy explains your first assignment. "We want you to learn how desktop publishing software works. Rudi, our graphic artist, will give you a software tour right away to help you begin working with desktop publishing software. You will also need to know the terms we use in this business. We will help you with that. Rudi will help you learn important graphics and layout skills. Leslie, our editor, will help you learn editing skills. When you have graphics and editing skills, we will be able to improve our products and serve the customers better. Let's go! Now is a good time to introduce you both to Rudi."

Rudi has just turned on the computer and is checking to make certain the mouse is connected. Rudi shakes hands with you and Stan. Then she shows you the mouse. "This is a new mechanical mouse we've just installed," she explains. "The **mouse** is a device that moves the pointer on the screen and is used to make selections from the various menus. The mouse has a ball on the bottom. When you move the mouse over a desk or other surface, it rolls the ball.

"We use a special mat, called a **mouse pad**, for the mouse. The mouse pad is designed to make the ball roll easily. When the ball rolls, it moves the pointer to a new location on the screen.

"By **clicking** or pressing a button on top of the mouse, you make selections that tell the computer what you want to do next. When there is more than one button, usually you click the left button to make a selection. Want to try it?"

You and Stan look at each other. "Yes," Stan replies.

Then Rudi pulls two chairs over to the front of the computer. "Here, sit down and I'll give you a guided tour.

"First you need to turn on the computer. Do you know how to start a computer with a hard disk?"

"No," Stan admits. "I've only used computers with floppy disk drives so far. Isn't it the same?"

"Not necessarily," Rudi explains. "If you have a hard drive, the computer can boot from system files on the hard disk. You don't need a floppy disk to start the computer. But we always want you to store your work on a floppy disk. This lets us use the space on the hard disk for program files. I'll turn on the switch. Watch the drive light on the hard drive."

Sure enough, the hard disk drive whirs, its light flashes, and the computer is ready to go to work.

Rudi shows you a copy of the software manual. "The manual is an important part of the software package," she explains. "I use it often to answer questions about the software."

Fill in the Work Assignment Log. Write the dates assigned and due dates for Chapter 1 work assignments. You will find the Work Assignment Log at the end of the chapter.

Name _____ Date _____ Period _____

SOFTWARE CHECK

Look up the following terms in your software manual. Use both the table of contents and the index to find the information you need. Write a short definition or description of each item.

Name of software: _____

_____

Menu, pull down: _____

_____

Select from a menu: _____

_____

Icon: _____

_____

Page view or show page: _____

_____

Save: _____

_____

Scroll bar: _____

_____

FACT SHEET: DESKTOP PUBLISHING SOFTWARE

- Many desktop publishing software programs require a hard disk. The hard disk is needed because these programs are too large and/or too complex to work efficiently from a floppy disk.

- Desktop publishing software usually requires the computer to work with several files at a time. For example, the desktop publishing software may need to combine several graphic and text files. This is another reason why hard disks are needed for many desktop publishing programs.

- Many menus have submenus or **dialog boxes** that require making additional selections. You are probably familiar with menus and submenus from your experience with word processing. You may not be familiar with the term *dialog box*. A dialog box is a boxed message from the program that asks for additional information.

- With some desktop publishing programs, it is possible to enter commands by using only keystrokes. However, using a mouse is usually faster.

- Many desktop publishing software packages have **pull-down menus**. The titles of these menus are usually listed at the top of the screen. To use a pull-down menu, move the pointer to the menu title. If you are using a mouse, point at the item you want and press, or click, the mouse button to select the item. If you want to cancel the choice you made, press the button a second time to **deselect**, or cancel, the item. Most desktop publishing software packages use **icons**, or small pictures, that represent choices such as pointing, entering text, drawing boxes, etc.

- With desktop publishing software, you view the page through a frame or **window**. You can move the page in the window with the **scroll bars**. Scroll bars are usually at the side and bottom of the screen. They function in a manner similar to scrolling or viewing different parts of a document in a word processing program. With some programs you can **enlarge** or reduce what you see in the window (that is, you can make the image appear larger or smaller).

AT THE EDITOR'S DESK

Rudi says, "Leslie has just arrived. He is our editor. Aiko and Andy want you to learn some basic editing techniques from him so you can help the customers. Let's go! I'll introduce you. Les, here are our new employees who need to learn about editing. Do you have time for a quick lesson?"

"Sure," says Leslie. "We can start with making copy more specific."

Leslie explains that one job of an editor is to make the text forceful, specific, interesting, and energetic. One way to do this is to cut out unnecessary words. In everyday speech and writing, people use many more words than are necessary for clear communication. There are three easy ways to strengthen the text files you edit. First, use short words instead of long ones. Second, replace over-used phrases with single words where possible. Third, use as few words as you can while keeping the meaning.

Here are some examples of words and phrases that can be replaced with shorter words and phrases. Review these examples carefully. Appendix A contains a list of phrases that can be made more **concise** (that is, expressed in fewer words or made more specific).

Replace This:	**With This:**
1. so that	so, to
2. despite the fact that	although, even though
3. seldom ever	seldom
4. delete out	delete
5. in advance of	before
6. in a timely manner	on time
7. as per our conversation	we discussed
8. thanks in advance	thanks
9. subsequent to	after
10. in the vicinity of	near
11. inside of	within
12. by the name of	named
13. a small number of	a few
14. on account of	because
15. give you a call	call
16. enclosed please find	enclosed is
17. filled to capacity	full

Leslie shows you his chart of **proofreaders' marks**. There is a copy of the chart in Appendix A. These marks are special codes that editors use to show how copy should be changed. If you learn a few marks at a time, you will soon know them all. Here are two proofreaders' marks to use in your first editing activities.

Proofreaders' Marks

⌐ Use this symbol to delete ~~out~~ words or characters.

∧ Use this symbol ∧(to) insert words or characters.

Name _____ Date _____ Period _____

YOU, THE EDITOR!

Practice making text more specific by completing the following exercises. When you finish, write the date in the "Date Completed" column of your Work Assignment Log.

PART 1   REWRITING PHRASES

Instructions: Column A contains five phrases. In the blanks in Column B, write more concise words or phrases that mean the same thing.

Column A	Column B
1. a large percentage of	1. _____
2. at an early date	2. _____
3. during the time that	3. _____
4. was of the opinion that	4. _____
5. give assistance to	5. _____

PART 2   EDITING TEXT

Instructions: Leslie has asked you to edit a course introduction for a customer. Read the following paragraphs carefully. Then replace or eliminate all unnecessary words or phrases. Some phrases may need to be reworded or rearranged. Long sentences should be made into two or more shorter ones. Remember to use proofreaders' marks for adding and deleting words. Use the list of proofreaders' marks in Appendix A as a reference.

```
            INTRODUCTION TO A COURSE


    Many of the exercises in this course are designed so
that they will give you a variety of opportunities to develop
editing skills.  Subsequent to your completion of all the
desktop publishing and editing exercises, you will be ready
for employment in a graphics field.  Inside of two months of
starting a full-time job, you will be a valuable employee
```

Continued

11

despite the fact that you will have had only one short course in desktop publishing.

In order for you to derive the maximum benefit from the instructional program, it is essential that you complete all assignments in a timely manner and turn them in at the termination of the class period each day.

Despite the fact that all of our equipment is not as modern as it could be, you will enjoy this class. Learning by doing can be fun.

Name _____ Date _____ Period _____

EXPLORING DESKTOP PUBLISHING

Complete the DTP activities. When you finish each activity, write the date in the "Date Completed" column of your Work Assignment Log. By completing these activities, you will learn how to:

- Start the computer.
- Load the desktop publishing software.
- Recognize and correctly name the parts of the working screen.
- Exit from the desktop publishing software.

DTP ACTIVITY 1A   GETTING STARTED

Instructions: Use your software manual as a reference to help you fill in the blanks.

Steps to start the computer: _____
_____

Steps to load the software: _____
_____

Steps to exit from the software: _____
_____

DTP ACTIVITY 1B   EXPLORING THE WORKING SCREEN

Instructions: As you watch a demonstration or use your software, sketch the parts of the working screen in the box that is provided. Use lines, circles, and rectangles. Label the parts. Make notes to help you remember details about each part. Write your notes in the margins or on a separate sheet of paper. Identify these items:

Page area
Menu bar
Dialog boxes
Mouse pointer
Pull-down menus
Title bar
Cursor
Scroll bars
Tool box
Rulers
Icons
Other items for your software

Working Screen

DTP ACTIVITY 1C EXPLORING SUBMENUS AND DIALOG BOXES

Instructions: Fill in the blank boxes with information you see in submenus and dialog boxes or print the screen if possible. Divide the boxes into smaller rectangles if necessary. Be sure to label each menu and dialog box.

Submenu: _____ Submenu: _____

Dialog Box: _____

Name _____ Date _____ Period _____

VOCABULARY REVIEW

vo-cab-u-lary

The following terms are used in Chapter 1 and are defined in the Glossary. Match the definitions to the terms by placing the letter of the correct definition in the space provided. Review Chapter 1 or the Glossary for any terms you do not remember. Not all definitions will be used.

Terms	Definitions
____ 1. mouse	A. a message asking for more information
____ 2. proofreaders' marks	B. pressing the mouse button to select
____ 3. clicking	C. to increase size
____ 4. concise	D. moves a pointer on the screen
____ 5. deselect	E. frames the page
____ 6. dialog box	F. said in fewer words
____ 7. pull-down menu	G. pictures that represent choices
____ 8. enlarge	H. a surface on which to operate a mouse
____ 9. window	I. to cancel or turn off a selection
____ 10. icons	J. a list of choices
	K. symbols showing copy changes

TREASURE HUNT

How long has it been since you went on a treasure hunt? As you learn about desktop publishing, you will go on a quest for certain items that will add to your knowledge about the subject. Save the items you collect by putting them in your publishing handbook.

For your first treasure hunt, visit a copy shop in your community or clip ads from newspapers or magazines. Collect these treasures:

- A list of the services provided with the prices charged.
- An order form.
- Tip sheets or guides for preparing materials for photocopy.
- If the copy shop has desktop publishing services, find out what hardware and software they use.

WORK ASSIGNMENT LOG

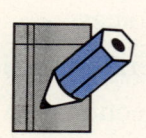

Fill in the "Date Assigned" and "Date Due" columns for each assignment that your teacher makes. When you complete an assignment, enter the date in the "Date Completed" column.

Chapter 1 Work Assignments	Date Assigned	Date Due	Date Completed
Software Check			
You, the Editor! Part 1			
You, the Editor! Part 2			
DTP Activity 1A			
DTP Activity 1B			
DTP Activity 1C			
Vocabulary Review			
Treasure Hunt			

Turn in Chapter 1 assignments after you have completed all of them, or follow your teacher's instructions. When these assignments are returned to you, put them in your publishing handbook.

CHAPTER 2
YOUR FIRST DESKTOP PUBLICATION

CHAPTER OBJECTIVES

When you have completed this chapter, you will be able to:

✓ Set the margins.

✓ Import and place both text and graphics.

✓ Save and print a page.

✓ Edit text by removing clichés and by proofreading more effectively.

INTRODUCTION

"Well hello!" exclaims Andy Koyama. "I'm glad to see you came back for the second day. I guess we didn't overpower you with all the information we gave you. This is a growing business and there will be opportunities for you if you decide to become a full-time employee when you finish school.

"Counting full-time and part-time, we now have 15 employees working at Omega Desktop. I send a special memo to employees once a year. It reminds those who have been working here for some time, as well as new employees, about the benefits of working for Omega. After you finish the work that Rudi and Leslie have for you, you will be able to update and print the memo so it can be sent out again."

When Rudi arrives, you and Stan say hello and then follow her into her office. "While Leslie is busy, I can show you how to use the desktop publishing software to combine illustrations with text. Omega is growing so fast that Mrs. Koyama thinks the employees should have some tips on answering the telephone. She has asked me to prepare this page of telephone procedures. I have found a picture of a telephone in some clip art. Now we need to combine the picture and the text and make a print of the page."

Stan asks, "What is clip art?" Rudi explains that **clip art** is the name for illustrations that are found in books or in software packages. Clip art pictures are made by artists for use by anyone who buys the books or software. These ready-made pictures can be used to illustrate desktop publications. The pictures can be used unchanged or they can be modified.

"Let's go!" Rudi says. "You can start the computer and I'll show you how to make the page of phone tips. Watch closely so you can do it later." Rudi asks you to turn on the computer. Then she gives Stan the job of starting the desktop publishing software. Stan whispers to you, "I'm glad I have the notes I made when Rudi showed us how to do this!" When the program is loaded, Rudi puts the disk containing Mrs. Koyama's text and clip art into the disk drive.

"First we need to make sure the page we are using is set up correctly," Rudi says. She shows you how to select the **page orientation**—the direction that the printing will appear on the paper—from the software menu. Page orientation can be vertical (tall) or horizontal (wide). Rudi tells you that not all desktop publishing software can print both vertical and horizontal pages. A vertical orientation is sometimes called portrait. **Portrait** means the page is taller than it is wide, like the picture of someone's face. A horizontal page orientation is sometimes called landscape. **Landscape** means the page is wider than it is tall, like a picture of a meadow or a desert.

Next Rudi shows you how to see where the margins are set. Most software programs have preset margins called **default margins**. A common default is one inch on each side and at the top and the bottom of the page. Rudi changes the left and right margins to $1\frac{1}{4}$ (1.25) inches.

"Now we can import the text file. **Importing files** means bringing them into a publication," Rudi says. "The filename is PHONEDOC. I'll select it from this menu. Watch and you will see the text appear on the screen." Sure enough, in just a few seconds, the type appears. Rudi shows you how to move the text on the page so there will be room for the clip art telephone picture. Then she centers the title above the text.

Rudi points to a line in the text that needs to be changed. She shows you how to take out the words that must be removed and how to type in the new information.

Next, Rudi chooses the picture file PHONEPIC from a list of the files on the disk. You and Stan are surprised by how quickly the picture appears on the screen.

Rudi points at the picture and selects the graphic. Then she centers it above the title. When the graphic is positioned correctly, she saves the page as a file, and then prints the page. It is always a good idea to save your work before you try to print, in case something goes wrong on the way to the printer.

You check to see if the printer has been turned on. Sure enough, it is ready to make a copy. Soon after Rudi selects the print function from the menu, you hear the printer go to work, and you know the copy is being made. Both you and Stan are eager to see the finished print. Rudi hands it to you, smiling. "Would you like to try to make the same page?" she asks. "It will be your first desktop publication!"

Fill in the Work Assignment Log. Write the dates assigned and due dates for Chapter 2 work assignments. You will find the Work Assignment Log at the end of the chapter.

Name _____ Date _____ Period _____

SOFTWARE CHECK

Find out how to perform the following functions with the software you are using. Look in the software manual or at the guidesheet your teacher gives you. Write the menu name or keystrokes you must use to perform each function. You will learn how to do each of the following operations when you complete DTP Activity 2A.

Select page orientation: _____
_____

Set margins (left, right, top, bottom): _____
_____

Change the type used: _____
_____

Load a text file: _____
_____

Center text: _____
_____

Revise text: _____
_____

Load a graphic file: _____
_____

Move a graphic: _____
_____

Save the publication: _____
_____

Print the publication: _____
_____

FACT SHEET: IMPORTING TEXT AND GRAPHICS

- Text and graphic files can be created with many different software packages. The files may be stored in different formats. Not all files can be imported and used with your desktop publishing software. You must find out which file formats can be used with your programs. This information is found in the manual for your software.

- Word processing files may contain special **formatting codes** that tell the printer how to print the text file. For example, centering codes will cause the printer to center a line of text. Other codes may cause the printer to print a word in boldface or to underline it. You should not be surprised if your DTP software ignores these special codes. In fact, many times it is easier to create a text file for desktop publishing without any special formatting codes. After you import the file into your desktop publishing program, you can format it.

- One important advantage of desktop publishing software is that it allows you to see on the screen exactly how the finished product will look. This capability is called **WYSIWYG** (pronounced "wizzy-wig") for "**What You See Is What You Get.**" When you import and format text, for example, letters, words, and paragraphs are displayed exactly as they will appear on your printout. In the same way, most graphics will be displayed as they will look when printed.

- When you save a publication that combines text and graphic files, your DTP software makes a new file (or files) for it. Some DTP software puts special extensions on the filenames, such as .PUB or .CHP. What happens to the original text and graphic files you used? In many cases, they will be unchanged and you can use them again in other documents.

AT THE EDITOR'S DESK

Leslie has some tips on editing for you. He is waiting for you in his office now. When you and Stan arrive, Leslie gives you another editing lesson. This is an important one. Leslie says that when you are working with customers, you must watch for clichés. A **cliché** is an expression that has been used over and over again until it sounds lifeless and dull. Clichés are sometimes wordy as well as worn out. Omega customers do not always know when they are using clichés. Your job is to help them edit their copy so it sounds lively and fresh.

Here are some examples of clichés:

as old as the hills
sink or swim
poor as a church mouse
last but not least
the bottom line
enclosed please find
we would like to take this opportunity to

You can think of other clichés. Several are listed in Appendix A. You will have the opportunity to edit copy for clichés.

Another important area of editing is proofreading. **Proofreading** means to check written work for grammar and punctuation errors, misspelled words, incorrect names or numbers, and words or sentences that have been left out. The following proofreading tips will help you when you proofread copy.

Proofreading Tips
1. Get someone else to proofread your work. It is very difficult to find your own typing and spelling errors.
2. Transposed and missing letters are two of the most common typing and spelling errors.
3. Missing spaces between words and missing punctuation marks are also common mistakes.
4. Always check the spelling of names used in articles or books.
5. Check the spelling of any words you do not know.
6. It is easy to overlook errors when proofreading on a computer screen. Therefore, always check the final version from a hard copy. Use a spell check program, if available.
7. Material should be proofread at least two times, once for continuity and meaning and once for typing, spelling, and format errors.
8. Proofread one line at a time using a ruler or other guide to help you focus on the line you are proofreading.
9. Proofread highly technical material with a partner. One of you can read from the original copy while the other partner checks the new copy against what is being read.
10. Proofread for grammar and punctuation.

Here are two more proofreaders' marks you can use. Look in Appendix A for a complete list of proofreaders' marks.

Proofreaders' Marks

⌒ Use this symbol to close up the text.

\# Use this symbol to add a space.

Name _____ Date _____ Period _____

YOU, THE EDITOR!

PART 1   WRITING CLICHÉS

Instructions: In the blanks, write at least five clichés that you hear often.

1. _____
2. _____
3. _____
4. _____
5. _____

PART 2   EDITING LETTERS

Instructions: Mr. Jerome, one of Omega's regular customers, has created two letters and saved them on a disk. He has asked you to help him edit the letters before he prints them. Try to remove all the clichés without changing the meaning. Watch for misspelled words and other errors. Make your corrections on the printed copies. Be sure to use standard proofreaders' marks.

(Date)

Ms. Beatriz Arroyo
Scandinavian Cruise Lines
2428 Palm Beach Drive
Miami, FL   33285

Dear Ms. Arroyo

I would like to take this opportunity to thank you for the courtesies you extended to me when I sailed on the <u>Stockholm</u> last week. This was the trip of a lifetime for Mrs. Jerome and me.

It could well have turned into a disaster when our travelers checks were stolen in San Juan. If you hadn't taken the bull by the horns and loaned us money on behalf of the steamship company, our long-awaited vacation would have been ruined.

Enclosed please find a check for $700.00 made out to Scandinavian Cruise Lines. This is a repayment of the money

Continued

loaned to us by your company. If the bottom line with your
firm is "no service too small--the customer is always right,"
I can testify to the fact that you live up to your slogan.
Thanks again.

Sincerely

James Jerome

(Date)

Mr. Anthony Marelli
Data Surveys, Inc.
3434 Avenue of the Americas
New York, NY 10291

Dear Tony

Per our conversation of the 23rd, I am sending a copy of the
year-end sales figures for Jerome Associates. After you have
had an opportunity to massage the data, I will give you a
call to see what you have come up with.

Our bottom line is we must show a profit for January if we
are to secure the loan fromthe Ridgecrest Bank. Thanks in
advance for lending a hand with our end-of-the-month reports.

Sincerely

James Jerome

PART 3 EDITING ANDY'S MEMO

Instructions: Leslie asks if you are ready to try your hand at editing Andy's yearly benefits memo. It has never been edited before, so it will need a lot of work. The first thing to do is to read the memo carefully and change any incorrect information. Also, Omega now provides dental benefits, so you will need to add the following information to the list of benefits available for full-time employees:

```
Dental - Employees and their dependents have up to $1,000
each in dental benefits each year.
```

Keep in mind that Andy does not always write as concisely as he should. Eliminate clichés and other unnecessary words. Proofread carefully. Key in the updated memo and print a copy. Save the file as MEMO1. If you are using a template disk, update the file named MEMO1 and save your changes. Print a copy of the file.

```
To:         All Omega Employees
From:       Andy Koyama, General Manager
Subject:  Employee Benefits

I would like to take the opportunity to describe the Omega
benefits program.  Omega Copies, Inc., is a dynamic, fast-
growing business.  We now employee 13 people--nine full-time
and four part-time.  We believe that Omega is a great place
to work and offers many opportunities.  Part-time employees
who perform well will be given first consideration for full-
time employment as openings occur or new positions are
created.

The following benefits are available for full-time employees:

Vacation - After one year of service and for every year
thereafter, each employee receives two weeks of paid
vacation.  Vacation requests must be approved in advance by
me.

Medical - Each employee, as well as his or her dependents,
receives medical coverage that includes hospital benfits,
doctors' fees, and laboratory fees.  The medical policy pays
80 percent of the cost of treatment, hospital stays, surgery,
etc.
The policy also has a $100 deductible clause.  This means you
```

Continued

pay the first $100 of your medical expenses. After that, the
policy pays 80 percent of the charges and you pay the rest.
Please see me for claim forms. All claims should be
submitted in a timely manner.

Sick Leave - Employees also get 12 days of paid sick leave
for the year--one day for each month. This time is to be
used by the employee only when he or she is sick. Sick leave
may also be used for bereavement provided the deceased is a
close relative.

Profit Sharing - Each employee recieves 1/2 of one percent of
each year's profit.

Medical claim forms are available in my office. The acid
test of how well anything works is in the using. The "proof
of the pudding," so to speak. Last but not least, please let
me know if you have any problems, either with processing
claim forms or needing more information.

Name _____ Date _____ Period _____

EXPLORING DESKTOP PUBLISHING

Practice combining text and graphics on a page. By completing the following DTP activities, you will learn how to:

- Set margins.
- Import and place text and graphics.
- Center text and make text bold.
- Make minor revisions to text.
- Save and print a page.

DTP ACTIVITY 2A   PREPARING THE PHONE TIPS PAGE

Instructions: Rudi has prepared the telephone procedures page requested by Mrs. Koyama. She asks you to go through the steps to produce a similar page. She explains that this exercise will help you to become more familiar with the DTP software. Observe a demonstration on how to prepare the page, or review the manual for your software. Fill in the blanks and then use your notes to repeat the process on your own. Rudi's sample telephone procedures page is at the end of this activity. Use it as a guide to prepare your own phone tips page.

1. Load the software. What command or action do you use? _____
   _____

2. Open a new document file. To make certain your work is saved as a new document named PHONEPRO, follow these steps:
   _____
   _____
   _____

3. Set the margins. Set up new page margins to leave $1\frac{1}{4}$ (1.25) inches on each side and one inch at the top and bottom by:
   _____
   _____
   _____

4. Change the type used to Times, Dutch, or Serif by: _____
   _____

5. Load a text file. Import the text file PHONEDOC by: _____
   _____
   _____

   If you are not using a template disk, key the text from Rudi's sample page. You will find it at the end of this activity.

6. Move the text file. Move the text file down so that the top line is two inches from the top by:
   _____
   _____
   _____

7. Center text. Center the title, "Omega Desktop, Inc. Telephone Procedures" on two lines by:
   _____
   _____

8. Make the title bold. Change the title to boldface type by: _____
   _____

9. Delete copy. Remove the phrase *(your name)* by: _____
   _____
   _____

10. Add copy. Type in your name after *This is* by: _____
    _____

11. Load the graphic. Import the graphic file PHONEPIC by: _____
    _____
    _____

    If you are not using a template disk, use the clip art PHONEPIC in Appendix B.

12. Move the graphic. Select and move the phone image to center it above the text by:
    _____
    _____
    _____

13. Save the publication. Save your work to disk by: _____
    _____
    _____

14. Print the publication. Print the PHONEPRO document by: _____
    _____

15. Exit from the software. End your session by: _____
    _____
    _____
    _____

OMEGA DESKTOP, INC.
TELEPHONE PROCEDURES

Please answer the telephone promptly. Your telephone manner can win or lose customers! This is what you should say when you answer:

> "Omega Desktop,
> Good morning! (or afternoon)
> This is (your name).
> How may I help you?"

If customers have questions you cannot answer, politely ask them to wait while you get the answer from someone else.

Before you leave the phone, press the red hold button and put the receiver back on the hook. DON'T FORGET to return to the customer as soon as possible.

If you take a message for a staff member who is not available to take a call, use our telephone note pads. WRITE LEGIBLY! Remember to sign your name and write the date and time. Give the note to the staff member or put it in his or her message holder.

During business hours, you may use the telephone for personal calls only in emergencies. Make your call as short as possible. Remember, we could lose an order while you are on the line.

All of the staff will benefit if Omega is successful. Your telephone manner can help!

DTP ACTIVITY 2B   PUBLISHING ANDY'S MEMO

Instructions: After you have completed the telephone procedures page, you will be able to desktop-publish Andy's memo to the employees on your own. You will create a DTP file named ANDYMEMO. Then you will import or load an existing text file into the DTP file. Refer to the notes you made in Activity 2A for information that you might need. Complete the following steps:

1. Load the DTP software.
2. Open a new DTP file. Give it a new name by saving it as ANDYMEMO.
3. Set the page margins to one inch on all sides.
4. Change the type used to Times, Dutch, or Serif.
5. Import the text file, MEMO1.
6. Move the text down so the first line is two inches from the top.
7. Make bold the headings *Vacation*, *Medical*, *Dental*, *Sick Leave*, and *Profit Sharing*.
8. Save the publication.
9. Print a proof copy.
10. Exit from the software.

Name _____ Date _____ Period _____

VOCABULARY REVIEW

vō-cab-u-lary

The following terms are used in Chapter 2 and are defined in the Glossary. Match the definitions to the terms by placing the letter of the correct definition in the space provided. Review Chapter 2 or the Glossary for any terms you do not remember. Not all definitions will be used.

Terms

____ 1. clip art
____ 2. cliché
____ 3. portrait
____ 4. landscape
____ 5. WYSIWYG
____ 6. proofreading
____ 7. import
____ 8. orientation
____ 9. default margins
____ 10. formatting codes

Definitions

A. to bring files into a publication
B. a vertical page layout
C. can be vertical or horizontal
D. the screen displays exactly what will print
E. ready-made graphic files or prints
F. name of a desktop publishing software package
G. an overused expression
H. tell the printer how to print the files
I. a horizontal page layout
J. preset features of the software
K. checking text for errors

TREASURE HUNT

Plan ahead! In the next chapter, you will format text and graphic files. Have you been looking at formats lately? One of the best ways to develop an eye for good page layout and design is to study the designs that others use. Start collecting examples of work that might be possible with desktop publishing. Here are some ideas:

- Find magazines and newspaper advertisements that are attractive and that might be possible with desktop publishing.
- Look for "junk mail" advertisements that are appealing combinations of text and graphic elements.
- Be prepared to show the examples you find to the class and to explain why you like them.
- Look for advertisements, flyers, or other promotional publications that are not appealing. Be prepared to share them with the class and to discuss why you do not like them.

WORK ASSIGNMENT LOG

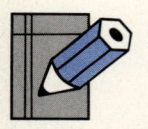

Fill in the "Date Assigned" and "Date Due" columns for each assignment that your teacher makes. When you complete an assignment, enter the date in the "Date Completed" column.

Chapter 2 Work Assignments	Date Assigned	Date Due	Date Completed
Software Check			
You, the Editor! Part 1			
You, the Editor! Part 2			
You, the Editor! Part 3			
DTP Activity 2A			
DTP Activity 2B			
Vocabulary Review			
Treasure Hunt			

Turn in Chapter 2 assignments after you have completed all of them, or follow your teacher's instructions. When these assignments are returned to you, put them in your publishing handbook.

CHAPTER 3
WORKING WITH TEXT AND GRAPHICS

CHAPTER OBJECTIVES

When you have completed this chapter, you will be able to:

✓ Use thumbnail sketches to plan a page layout.

✓ Use rulers to guide the placement of text and graphics.

✓ Set margins and place text and graphics according to the layout.

✓ Break text into blocks and insert a graphic into the text.

✓ Make editorial changes in the text with the DTP software.

✓ Edit copy to eliminate redundancies.

INTRODUCTION

Rudi is busy preparing a layout for a new job. She has a deadline to meet. She shows you the stack of work orders waiting on her desk. "I'm glad you and Stan are here to help me," she says. "Here is an urgent report that must be completed and mailed to Omega stockholders. Andy wants to include a graphic showing how the business has grown."

Rudi suggests that first you decide on the page layout. The layout should show where each part of the report will go. When Rudi plans a new page layout, she makes **thumbnail sketches**. These are small drawings that show roughly where blocks of text and graphics might be placed on the page. Rudi quickly draws several small vertical rectangles on a sheet of paper. "Now," she explains, "let's consider what needs to go on the page. You need to lay out Andy's text and the graphic. He wants to print the report on the new Omega letterhead that I designed. Try drawing different arrangements of the parts in thumbnail sketches."

Rudi discusses each part of the layout. "First let's decide what margins to use. The letterhead has the Omega logo at the top. It will require about two inches of space. Now we need to think about where the graphic might go. We have at least three options. We could put it under the logo and above the body of the letter. We could put the body of the letter above the graphic. However, if you read Andy's letter, you'll see that he has mentioned the graphic in the fourth paragraph. Placing it in the text below the fourth paragraph might be better yet. I always try to place any illustration as close as I can to the text it illustrates. This helps the reader."

With this layout you must use another feature of the DTP software to insert a graphic into a block of text. This feature is one that you will use often. Rudi asks you to set up the page orientation and margins according to the layout you have planned. After you import the text file, Rudi shows you how to turn on the rulers so they are displayed on the screen. The **rulers** are guides that help you place the text and graphics.

You can select the text and move it down to leave exactly two inches at the top for the letterhead.

Next Rudi shows you how to divide the text to make room for the graphic file. "This operation is different with each DTP software program, so watch closely," she says. "Take notes because I want you to do it later on your own."

The graphic is too large to fit in the layout. Rudi shows you how to select the graphic and make it smaller. Then she moves it into the space below the fourth paragraph in Andy's letter.

Now the rest of the letter can be placed under the graphic. Rudi flows the text into the space at the bottom of the page. Leslie has made a few editorial revisions to the text. He has given you the marked-up copy. Rudi asks you to make these changes before printing a proof on the Omega letterhead. A **proof** is copy printed for checking a layout for changes needed before printing the final copy.

Rudi demonstrates how to revise the text. She moves the mouse pointer to the first place in the text where Leslie has made changes. When she clicks the mouse button, an insertion point appears. An **insertion point** is a marker that shows where keystrokes will appear when new wording is added. Rudi coaches as you make the other changes.

"Okay, you are ready to go to press! Remember to save the file before you print. Use a piece of blank paper for a proof copy. This copy will tell you how the printed page looks as it is set up in the DTP software. When you are satisfied with the results, I'll give you the new letterhead for a final proof that Andy can review."

Fill in the Work Assignment Log. Write the dates assigned and due dates for Chapter 3 work assignments. You will find the Work Assignment Log at the end of the chapter.

Name _____ Date _____ Period _____

SOFTWARE CHECK

Can you do the following operations with the DTP software you are using? If so, what menu or method do you use? Remember to refer to the software manual, if necessary.

Can you turn on rulers? Horizontal? _____ Vertical? _____
Menu/method: _____
_____

Can you turn off the rulers? _____ Menu/method: _____
_____

Can you change the measurement to other scales? _____
Menu/method: _____
_____

What are the scales? _____

Can you create guidelines for positioning elements on the page? ____
How? _____
_____

Can you expand and shrink the space the text occupies? _____
How? _____
_____

Can you change the size of a graphic? _____ How? _____
_____
_____

Can you position a graphic at any place on the page? _____
How? _____
_____

Can you flow text around the graphic? _____ Menu/method: _____
_____
_____

39

FACT SHEET: LAYOUT TOOLS

- Thumbnail layout sketches are usually converted to full size layouts using a grid. A **grid** is a guide that shows the page margins and the locations of other elements that are likely to be the same on each page. In some DTP software, these elements include the page margins, the way the page is divided into columns, and other features. Grids are important for designing documents that have more than one page. Grids help give unity to multi-page layouts. Pages planned with the same grid appear as though they belong to the same publication.

- **Picas** and **points** are traditionally used for the precise measurement of type and typeset documents. There are six picas in an inch and 12 points in a pica, or 72 points in an inch. These measurements are used instead of inches for measuring the height and vertical spacing of type and the thickness of rules. Some DTP software programs even provide measurements in fractions of points. Centimeters and millimeters are also options for measuring with some DTP software.

- Remember, if you make editing changes or corrections to imported text with most desktop publishing software, these changes will not be made to the original word processing text file. If you use the same text file again, you must repeat the same corrections.

- When you are setting margins for a page, remember that most printers cannot print out to the edge of the paper. Printing to the edge is called a **bleed**. Copy machines have the same limitation. As a rule, you will want to leave a margin of at least $1/4$ (.25) to $1/2$ (.5) inch on all sides of the paper.

AT THE EDITOR'S DESK

"One of the things we do when we edit copy is to eliminate **redundancies**," Leslie says. He explains that a redundant phrase is one that contains unnecessary repetition. This repetition can be eliminated without loss of meaning. Appendix A contains a list of redundant phrases. Actually, eliminating redundancies makes your text more concise. Redundancies are another form of wordiness, as are clichés. For example, in "At the Editor's Desk" in Chapter 1, two of the wordy phrases, "delete out" and "filled to capacity," contain redundancies.

Here are some commonly used redundancies that should be eliminated or replaced with more precise expressions:

Redundant Phrase:	Replace With:
big in size	big, large
lift up	lift
eliminate altogether	eliminate
reduce or eliminate	reduce
commute to and from	commute
follow after	follow

Here is a sentence that contains wordiness and redundancies:

```
When you are commuting to and from your place of employment,
it is very important to be on time by arriving at the
appropriate time.
```

Here is a sentence that says the same thing in less space:

```
Always arrive at work on time.
```

Being able to identify misspelled words when you are proofreading is another important editing skill. Some words are misspelled by many people. It is especially important that you spell these words correctly because they are misspelled so often. Appendix A contains a list of frequently misspelled business words. Study these words until you are confident that you can spell them correctly. Be sure to check for these commonly misspelled words in all of your editing activities.

Here are two more proofreaders' marks to use in your editing assignments.

Proofreaders' Marks

∾ This mark means **transpose** or change the sequence of letters or words.

bf or a jagged line under a word means to type the word in **boldface**.

Name _____ Date _____ Period _____

YOU, THE EDITOR!

PART 1 EDITING A MEMO FOR REDUNDANCIES

Instructions: Leslie has a memo that Andy wants to send to employees. Andy uses more words than he should and always asks Leslie to edit his memos so they are concise, but informative. Leslie wants you to edit Andy's memo before it is printed and distributed to Omega employees.

- Watch for spelling and typographical errors.

- Remember to use the proofreaders' marks you have learned.

- If you are using a template disk, update the file named MEMO2. Load the file and make the corrections you have marked on your copy of the memo. Print the revised memo.

- If you are not using a template disk, key in the corrected copy. Give the file the name MEMO2. Print the memo.

```
To:   Omega Desktop employees
From: Andy Koyama
Subject:  Help Wanted

Here at Omega Desktop, Inc., we are expereincing quite a few
growing pains!  These growing pains have caused a tremendous
increase in our work load.  Most of the problems we are
dealing with come about because we can't get the work done in
a timely manner.  Many of the common problems we are
experiencing at Omega Desktop could probably be reduced, or
eleminated, if we would take the time to look for some more
qualified part-time employees.

That is the purpose of this memo, to let you know the
situation and to ask you if you know anyone who is interested
in part-time work and who has enough backgroun with computers
that they can learn on the job to do graphics, page layout,
and editing for our culstomers.  If so, please have them
contact me.
```

PART 2   EDITING AN ARTICLE

Instructions: Miss Jean Hayes, an amateur journalist and one of Omega's customers, wants you to proofread her work and make suggestions for improving it. Remember to make your corrections on hard copy first.

- Use standard proofreaders' marks to mark the copy.
- If you are using a template disk, update the file named KINGROCK. Save the updated file under the same name and print a copy.
- If you are not using a template disk, key in your corrected copy and print it. Save the document under the filename KINGROCK.

```
            THE KING OF ROCK IS BACK--WITH NEW PRIORITIES


    Santa Rosa--George Stevens made his reputation over ten

years ago with high voltage performances that, astonishingly,

turned his often brooding, downbeat songs about despair and

death into upbeat, life-affirming songs of joy.  Few

performers have ever exhibited such intensity and desire.

    But this morning, the king of rock in the late '70s and

early '80s is tiptoeing back and forth down the hall of a

comfortable hotel checking on his children (ages 2 and 4) who

are sleeping in another room.  His wife is out shopping.

    The rock star, now 43, has just reentered the pop world

after taking a six-year break in which he married, moved to

Scotland (the birthplace of his wife) and started raising a

family.  George Stevens has a new set of priorities this time

around.  He wants to perform, but he also wants to enjoy his
```

Continued

roles as husband and father. He interrupts the interview several times to check on Matthew, 4, and Erin, 2.

Though Stevens misses the States, he also plans to continue living in Scotland with his wife, Maraise Evans--who is an artist of some repute--and their two children. They are both very pleased about the third child they expect to arrive in three months. Stevens says he will continue to make albums, write songs, and make the occasional personal appearance, but he won't tour.

Won't tour? Sacrilege! Is this the same man who was so anxious to perform that he did his act in a full leg cast after breaking the leg in a 1980 fall from a platform on stage? Is this the same man who, in reflecting on his fall, says: "I just couldn't hold back. There was a moment when I felt I could fly and I just soared off the platform. It was a six-foot drop and I didn't land properly. I was aware of the danger. I had never tried the jump before. But something inside me just pushed me over.

Asked about the differences between the old George Stevens and the new one, he explains, "When you are young and single and a rock star, you have the luxury of being romantic about life and death. You can be frivolous. When you have a

Continued

loving partner and children, you have a responsibility to take care of yourself. You have to spend time with them. Children depend on you for everything. You can't be daydreaming about exploding like a fireball on stage. You have new priorities."

Stevens is one of several celebrated pop stars to take a sabbatical. Some of the breaks from the fast lane have been the result of legal or physical problems, but the tendency seems to be toward a voluntary respite--and the trend is likely to gain momentum as veteran artists see the time away from tours as both a means of revitalizing their art.

About his own decision to step away from the pop music world, Stevens says, "When you are on tour all the time, your life becomes a big swirl. Relationships with those you love become too intense or else lose all sense of intimate communication. You don't have time to step back and put everything in perspective."

Sabbaticals like George Stevens's are a sign of the maturing of rock. Recording stars used to be under tremendous pressure to keep turning out new singles and keep touring because rock music was considered a fad. The game plan was to get all you could while it lasted.

Continued

Things are different now. Rock has become a multibillion-dollar-a-year institution. Performers are starting to tell recording companies when to expect new releases rather than delivering them on a company timetable. Artists now think in terms of long careers. The thought of taking time off is no longer seen as "bad for business." In some cases, it makes good sense.

Stevens's case is especially interesting because his break was open-ended. He walked away without any promise to return. When asked if he has any regrets, George replies, "Regrets are futile--but no, I have none. It was right for me to walk away then just as it is right for me to be active again now. I feel stronger and healthier because of the break. I think my music is better than it was five years ago.

The fans certainly seem to agree. They gave Stevens continuous standing ovations for more than half his show at his first series of comeback performances. Weldome back George! We've missed you!

Name _____ Date _____ Period _____

EXPLORING DESKTOP PUBLISHING

Complete the following activities. When you finish, write the date in the "Date Completed" column in your Work Assignment Log.

DTP ACTIVITY 3A   LETTER TO OMEGA STOCKHOLDERS

Instructions: You are ready for your first desktop publishing assignment for Omega Desktop. It is time for Omega's management to send the quarterly letter to the stockholders telling them about the corporation's progress. Andy and Aiko have written the letter. Here is Leslie's edited copy of the letter. If you are not using a template disk, key this letter and name the file REPORT.TXT.

(Use today's date)

Dear Stockholder

This is your informal quarterly report on the progress of
Omega Desktop, Inc. (formerly Omega Copies, Inc.).

Since our last letter three months ago, we have expanded our
staff to include two new part-time employees. They were
needed to handle the increased number of duplication jobs
we've had and to free our graphic artist to assist customers
who wish to rent desktop publishing equipment.

Both of our new employees are also learning desktop
publishing skills. They will soon be assisting rental
customers. We feel the rental service will grow more
quickly if clients have the help they need to use the
equipment effectively.

In fact, our income figures for the past three months show
dramatic growth in rentals. The chart below shows how the
earnings from duplicating and from rentals compare.

We feel our decision to purchase equipment and expand into
the desktop publishing area was a wise one. We expect the
income from rentals to continue to grow.

Continued

49

```
If you have any questions or comments, please contact us.

Respectfully submitted



Andy Koyama              Aiko Koyama
General Manager          President
```

Rudi has given you these instructions:

1. Turn on the DTP software rulers. Set them to measure in inches.
2. Leave 2¼ (2.25) inches at the top for the Omega letterhead logo. Use 1¼ (1.25) inch margins on each side and a ¾ (.75) inch margin at the bottom.
3. Select Times, Dutch, or Serif as the type used. Import the text file named REPORTXT and place it according to the layout. Make the corrections shown on the edited copy.
4. Import the graphic file CHART3MO. Place it after the fourth paragraph of the letter. If you are not using a template disk, leave space after the fourth paragraph to paste in the graphic from Appendix B.
5. Save the publication file under the name STOCKLET.
6. Print a proof copy to check your layout.
7. When you are satisfied with the results, print a second proof on Omega letterhead for Andy and Aiko to review.

DTP ACTIVITY 3B   PUBLISHING ANDY'S MEMO

Instructions: Earlier you updated and printed a proof copy of Andy's memo about employee benefits. You named the DTP file ANDYMEMO. Now Andy wants you to print copies for each employee. To make the memo more attractive, add small graphic icons to illustrate each of the benefits. They are stored on the template disk under the filenames VACATION, MEDICAL, DENTAL, SICK, and PROFITS. If you are not using a template disk, use the clip art for these illustrations from Appendix B.

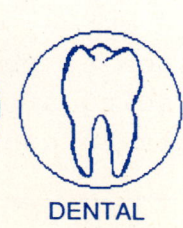

VACATION   MEDICAL   DENTAL   SICK   PROFITS

Follow these steps to prepare the final memo:

1. On a separate sheet of paper, draw at least four thumbnail sketches to plan the new layout. Indicate margins and placement of text and graphic elements.
2. Select the thumbnail layout you prefer. On the thumbnail sketch page, write why you chose the layout you selected.
3. Load the DTP software and change the page orientation and margins according to your layout. Use rulers and guidelines (if available) to aid in placement of text and graphics.
4. Import the text and graphic files. Adjust the text to make room for the illustrations. Place the illustrations according to your layout. Adjust the size of the graphics if necessary.
5. Save your revised DTP file, giving it the new name BENEFITS. Print a proof copy.
6. Examine the proof copy and adjust your layout as necessary. When you are satisfied with the results, print a final copy.

Name _____ Date _____ Period _____

VOCABULARY REVIEW

vo·cab·u·lary

The following terms are used in Chapter 3 and are defined in the Glossary. Match the definitions to the terms by placing the letter of the correct definition in the space provided. Review Chapter 3 or the Glossary for any terms you do not remember. Not all definitions will be used.

Terms

___ 1. pica
___ 2. point
___ 3. thumbnail sketch
___ 4. grid
___ 5. bleed
___ 6. insertion point
___ 7. proof
___ 8. redundancy
___ 9. transpose
___ 10. rulers

Definitions

A. a page guide locating margins and columns
B. to reverse the order
C. where keystrokes will appear when a text file is edited
D. displays measurements for locating elements on the page
E. words or phrases that can be eliminated without changing the meaning
F. to make something larger
G. a small drawing for experimenting with layouts
H. one-twelfth of a pica
I. a trial print for checking the layout
J. one-sixth of an inch
K. to print to the edge of the paper

TREASURE HUNT

Company logos are usually simple graphic designs intended to represent the company image. Collect company logos that you think convey an appropriate company image.

- Use sources such as magazines, newspapers, the yellow pages of the phone book, letterhead stationery, and product labels.

- If possible, visit a local business and ask for a copy of its logo. Find out the history and background of the logo.

WORK ASSIGNMENT LOG

Fill in the "Date Assigned" and "Date Due" columns for each assignment that your teacher makes. When you complete an assignment, enter the date in the "Date Completed" column.

Chapter 3 Work Assignments	Date Assigned	Date Due	Date Completed
Software Check			
You, the Editor! Part 1			
You, the Editor! Part 2			
DTP Activity 3A			
DTP Activity 3B			
Vocabulary Review			
Treasure Hunt			

Turn in Chapter 3 assignments after you have completed all of them, or follow your teacher's instructions. When these assignments are returned to you, put them in your publishing handbook.

CHAPTER 4
COMPARING PASTEUP TECHNIQUES

CHAPTER OBJECTIVES

When you have completed this chapter, you will be able to:

✔ Compare manual and computerized pasteup.

✔ Combine manual and computerized pasteup to create originals for photocopying.

✔ Enter text directly with the DTP software.

✔ Copy blocks of text.

✔ Edit to eliminate redundancies.

INTRODUCTION

Rudi's new office is ready. She now has a new and more powerful computer and new shelves for storing software and disks. On the wall there is a large bulletin board where she can display Omega products. The office is well lighted and has a large window next to the door so customers can watch Rudi at work.

You are surprised to see that Rudi has arranged some old tools carefully in her office. A T square and several metal triangles are hanging on the wall above a table with a glass top. There are jars of rubber cement and tape dispensers. A cup holds small brushes, several pens and pencils, and an X-ACTO® brand graphic art knife. Metal rulers hang on one hook and **plastic templates** for drawing circles and ellipses hang on another.

"Do you like it?" Rudi asks. Then she adds, "You'd be surprised how many old gadgets I've thrown away because I never use them anymore. However, I've kept some important tools that we still need for doing pasteup manually, without the computer." Rudi explains that the expression **pasteup** means attaching text and illustrations to a page by hand. Desktop publishing software imitates many of the old manual pasteup techniques. For example, guidelines in the DTP program are like the light-blue pencil guidelines that pasteup artists use for aligning text and graphic elements. The expression **cut-and-paste** means to assemble a page manually from cutout pieces of copy and text. Cut-and-paste also describes what is done when the cut (delete) and paste (insert) commands are used with DTP software.

"The computer is marvelous," Rudi says, "but sometimes it's faster to do part of the work by hand. And there are jobs that the computer hasn't learned to do yet! It's important to know a few simple pasteup techniques so that you can do the work your computer can't do."

Rudi shows you a mailer she is designing for a company. "They want some of the lettering on the cover set at an angle. We can't set text at an angle with the DTP software. So I will print the text on a separate sheet of paper and paste it up on the **original**, the page we will photocopy.

Comparing Pasteup Techniques

"Here's another example. Look at this nice ink drawing Aiko made for the new Omega price list. We could run Aiko's drawing through the scanner to make it into a graphic file. A **scanner** is a machine that reads a drawing or photograph and saves it as a computer file. If we scanned Aiko's drawing, the delicate lines wouldn't be as sharp. So I will paste up her drawing on the original instead."

Rudi describes another example. "This is a print of a large graphic. It took nearly 15 minutes to print. The customer wants the title changed. Instead of reprinting the whole thing, we can print a new title and paste it on this original in a few seconds."

Rudi gives you a job that requires manual pasteup. Omega has a new client who is starting a flying school. The flying school owner wants invitations made for an open house where customers can inspect the company's planes. She wants to use the company logo, but she does not have a graphic file for it. Instead, she has brought in several prints of the logo that you can paste on the originals for the invitation and its envelope. This project will also give you practice with entering text directly with the DTP software. Rudi will show you how to set up the invitation and the envelope when you are ready.

Fill in the Work Assignment Log. Write the dates assigned and due dates for Chapter 4 work assignments. You will find the Work Assignment Log at the end of the chapter.

Name _____ Date _____ Period _____

SOFTWARE CHECK

Can you perform the following operations with your DTP software? Check your software manual or the information sheet your teacher gives you. Then read the Fact Sheet information to help fill in the comparison chart.

Can your DTP software rotate type? _____ How? _____
_____

Can your DTP software rotate graphics? _____ How? _____
_____

Comparison of Pasteup Tools		
Operation	*Manual Pasteup Tools*	*DTP Tools*
Drawing guidelines		
Cutting out text or a graphic		
Aligning a text or graphic cutout		
Fastening the cutout to the page		

FACT SHEET: MANUAL PASTEUP TECHNIQUES

- To draw guidelines or write notes on a photocopy original, a **light-blue pencil** is used. The light-blue lines will not reproduce when the page is photocopied or photographed. Some layout sheets for pasting up originals have margins or grids printed on them in light-blue ink. On a color monitor, some DTP software programs show margins and guidelines in light blue.

- For some pasteup jobs, it is important to be able to remove parts of the original page and reuse them. Cutouts attached with wax can be removed easily. Wax can be applied to small cutouts with a wax stick. For larger jobs, a **waxer** is useful. It melts the wax and rolls it evenly onto the paper. Another way to attach cutouts temporarily is to put rubber cement on the back of the cutout only. To attach cutouts permanently, put rubber cement on both the back of the cutout and on the layout sheet.

- Remember that dirt will photocopy. Use a rubber cement pick-up to remove any exposed cement that might attract dirt. A **pick-up** is a chunk of dry rubber cement. Use it like an eraser to remove extra cement.

- **Stripping** is another manual technique for combining text and graphic cutouts. Stripping produces a single-layer master while pasteup produces a master with an overlay or two layers. Stripping is done on a light table. A **light table** is a table or box with a glass top. There are lights under the glass. The lights are bright enough to shine through two layers of paper. The lights are used to align text or graphics on two overlapping sheets of paper. The pasteup artist cuts out parts from each layer simultaneously and then tapes (strips) the parts together to make the original.

AT THE EDITOR'S DESK

Some writers think that long words (three or more syllables) are better than short words. They believe long words will impress people. Actually, long words sometimes seem forced and self-conscious. For most long words, there are shorter words that express the same thing. These shorter words communicate ideas quickly. They add vigor and vitality to the writing. A **synonym** is another word that has the same meaning.

Here are some examples of long words that have shorter synonyms.

delinquent	late
acquiesce	agree
terminate	end, fire
incinerate	burn
expeditiously	quickly
prevaricate	lie
individual	person
purchase	buy

One reason for using a word processor to create text files for DTP is that some of these programs have a built-in **thesaurus**. You can use the thesaurus to find synonyms that are shorter and more forceful. You can also use a printed thesaurus or a dictionary of synonyms, as well as the regular dictionary.

The editor's slogan must be: "Eliminate wordiness wherever possible." Wordiness means using several words where one or two will do, repeating information with no gain in meaning, or being complicated or awkward when you should be simple and direct.

Most documents have more words and more complicated sentences than they need. When you are editing a message for someone else to read, remember that reading requires time and energy. Delete unnecessary words. If there are several long, complex sentences, consider making them more readable by making them shorter and simpler. Keep or rephrase what you need to make the author's meaning clear and interesting to the reader. Delete everything else.

Example:

If you must be absent from the class in which you are enrolled, it will be your responsibility to get the assignment from another student in the class.

Revision:

If you miss class, get the assignment from a classmate.

Example:

Jim's supervisor, tired of his poor punctuality record, terminated his employment with the company.

Revision:

Jim was fired for excessive tardiness.

Here are two more proofreaders' marks to use in your editing assignments.

Proofreaders' Marks

stet — An editor's word meaning to leave it the way it was ~~before I changed it.~~ *stet*

/ *lc* This mark means to change Capital Letters into lowercase. *lc lc*

Name _____ Date _____ Period _____

YOU, THE EDITOR!

PART 1   FINDING SYNONYMS FOR LONGER WORDS

Instructions: Read the following list of two- to five-syllable words. Use a dictionary to look up the meaning of any words you do not understand. Write a short synonym for each word.

List of Words	**Synonyms**
1. inhabit	_____
2. vehicle	_____
3. sufficient	_____
4. approximately	_____
5. remittance	_____
6. remuneration	_____
7. domicile	_____
8. utilize	_____
9. beverage	_____
10. obsequious	_____
11. enlargement	_____
12. attempt	_____
13. supplement	_____
14. affirmative	_____
15. demonstrate	_____

PART 2   EDITING TO ELIMINATE WORDINESS

Instructions: On the next page is an article that a customer has submitted for a newsletter. Please edit the article using all necessary proofreaders' marks. Make the text as concise as you can. Remember, avoid using a two- or three-syllable word if a one-syllable word will do. Do not use a paragraph to say what you can say in one sentence.

MEAN MARY MORRIS

The most unforgettable character I ever met was the woman who lived next door to us when I was a child. Her house was very old and scary with a haunted appearance. Mary made her living by selling herbal remedies she prepared from plants she cultivated in her yard. I used to play in the yard a lot in the summer and the smell of Mean Mary's herbs would give the air a lovely fragrance.

We lived in a small, old house that looked a lot like Mary's except it wasn't scary. My mother liked our house because it was old but in good condition. My friedns used to come over to play in the summer because there were lots of trees to climb. Some of them gave a good view of Mean Mary's yard.

When she would look up and see us watching her from the trees, she would get as mad as fire and try to hit us with her broom. We would have to scramble up out of the way. Once, Brian, my best friend, fell out of the tree while she was swinging her broom. She chased him all the way home hitting him on the head and shoulders with her broom. That was when we gave her the name Mean Mary.

Continued

As we got older, Mary got meaner. She kept a shot gun wiht rock salt in it. If we so much as dared to put a foot on her property, she whould run out and threaten us with the gun. Fortunately, she never shot at any of us. The older she got, the more chrochety she became. She was the meanest person I ever knew.

Name　　　　　　　　　　　　Date　　　　Period

EXPLORING DESKTOP PUBLISHING

Practice combining manual and computer pasteup techniques in these activities. You will learn how to:

■ Enter text directly on a page.

■ Duplicate text and place the copy on the same page to print copies two to a page.

■ Manually paste a graphic onto a page you have desktop-published.

■ Print small labels with DTP software and use them for manual pasteup.

DTP ACTIVITY 4A   PREPARING INVITATIONS

Instructions: You are now ready to prepare invitations for the flying school owner that Rudi told you about earlier. Plan a layout to print the invitations **two-up**, or two on an $8^1/_2$ by 11-inch page. Your layout can be portrait or landscape, as shown in the thumbnail sketches. If possible, watch a demonstration that shows how to enter the invitation text and how to cut and paste the text for the second copy of the invitation. Take notes and use them to repeat the process on your own.

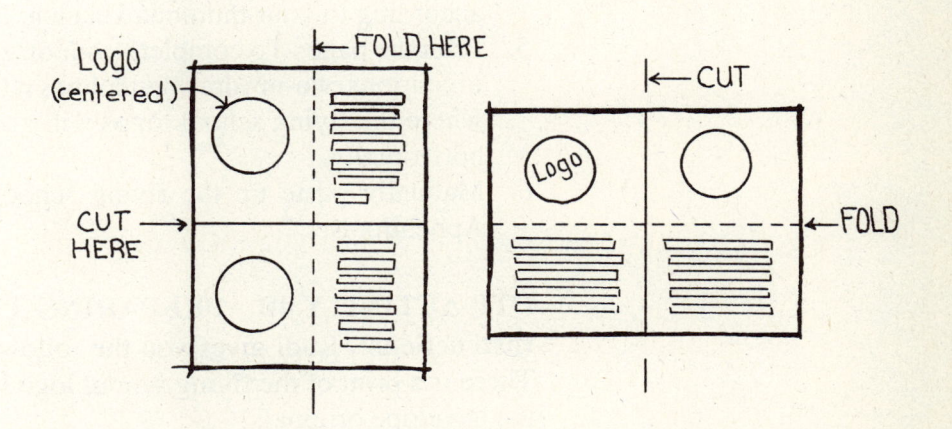

Follow these steps to prepare the invitations:

1. Load the DTP software and open a new file named INVIT2UP.
2. Set the margins according to the layout you have planned.
3. Change the type used to Helvetica, Swiss, or Sans Serif, then enter the text that follows on the next page.

> Wings for Rent is offering a new service: training for a private pilot's license. If you are interested in obtaining a flying license, you are invited to visit our facility at the Santa Rosa airport. Inspect our training planes and talk with our instructors between 9:00 a.m. and 5:00 p.m. on April 19.
>
> All visitors will be eligible to win one free hour of flight instruction that will be awarded in a drawing at the end of the day! You do not have to be present to win.
>
> Please call for more information.

4. Cut and paste the text to make a second copy and position it according to your thumbnail sketch.
5. Print the page. To complete your original page for reproducing the invitations two-up, draw guidelines with a light-blue pencil showing where the flying school logos will go. Center them vertically and horizontally.
6. Manually paste up the flying school logos. Use the copies in Appendix B.

DTP ACTIVITY 4B   PREPARING THE ENVELOPE

Instructions: Rudi gives you the following layout for the envelope. There is a print of the flying school logo in Appendix B to paste up on the envelope original.

Follow these steps to prepare the envelope original.

1. Load the file named LABELS into your DTP software and print one copy. If you are not using a template disk, use a copy of the TAKING OFF! label from Appendix B.
2. Open a new file named ENVELOPE. Use the same type you selected for the invitation. Enter and place the text for the return address as shown on Rudi's layout. The return address is:

Wings for Rent
453 Airport Road
Santa Rosa, CA 95401

3. Print the ENVELOPE file.
4. Using a light-blue pencil, mark the locations of the logo and the TAKING OFF! label on your print.
5. Paste up the Wings for Rent logo and the TAKING OFF! label to complete the original for the envelope.

Name _____ Date _____ Period _____

VOCABULARY REVIEW

vo-cab-u-lary

The following terms are used in Chapter 4 and are defined in the Glossary. Match the definitions to the terms by placing the letter of the correct definition in the space provided. Review Chapter 4 or the Glossary for any terms you do not remember. Not all definitions will be used.

Terms

_____ 1. light table
_____ 2. stripping
_____ 3. pick-up
_____ 4. paste up
_____ 5. plastic template
_____ 6. synonym
_____ 7. scanner
_____ 8. waxer
_____ 9. thesaurus
_____ 10. original

Definitions

A. tool for spreading heated wax on paper
B. page from which photocopies are made
C. helps find words with the same meaning
D. a word that sounds like another word
E. attaching parts of a page to an original
F. reads a picture and saves it as a graphic file
G. tool for removing excess rubber cement
H. a word that has the same meaning
I. used for aligning two layers of copy
J. tool for drawing shapes such as circles and boxes
K. combining parts of a page by cutting and taping the pieces

TREASURE HUNT

In the next chapter you will begin to study type. To prepare for this, collect at least ten examples of type from newspapers, magazines, "throwaway" publications, and other sources.

Try to find a variety of type from simple to very decorative. Look for type of all sizes. To begin your own type catalog, arrange the samples you collect on binder pages for your publishing handbook. Study your type samples and decide:

- Which are best for attracting attention?
- Which are easiest to read in body text?
- Which are best for short explanations in captions?
- Which seem to have special purposes?

Look for type you might use later in this course when you design the cover, set up the title page, and prepare the table of contents for your publishing handbook.

WORK ASSIGNMENT LOG

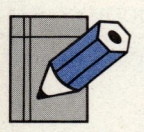

Fill in the "Date Assigned" and "Date Due" columns for each assignment that your teacher makes. When you complete an assignment, enter the date in the "Date Completed" column.

Chapter 4 Work Assignments	Date Assigned	Date Due	Date Completed
Software Check			
You, the Editor! Part 1			
You, the Editor! Part 2			
DTP Activity 4A			
DTP Activity 4B			
Vocabulary Review			
Treasure Hunt			

Turn in Chapter 4 assignments after you have completed all of them, or follow your teacher's instructions. When these assignments are returned to you, put them in your publishing handbook.

CHAPTER 5
WORKING WITH TYPEFACES

CHAPTER OBJECTIVES

When you have completed this chapter, you will be able to:

✓ Recognize common serif and sans serif typefaces.

✓ Print sample pages using different typefaces, styles, sizes, and leading.

✓ Select and specify type for appearance and readability.

✓ Proofread for and correct punctuation errors.

INTRODUCTION

Rudi asks you to help put a new poster on her office wall. It shows the alphabet in many **typefaces**. When the poster is up, Rudi explains what it is about. "This tells you about typefaces. Look at these Helvetica alphabets. Helvetica is a **type family**. It comes in several different faces. Helvetica, Helvetica Narrow, and Helvetica Outline are faces in the Helvetica family."

Each face comes in different **type styles**: the **normal** face, the **italic** or slanted face, the heavier **bold** face, and **bold italic**—a heavier slanted face. The type used to print each Helvetica style is called a **font**. For example, Helvetica Narrow Italic is one font. With some printers, a different font is required to print each size of Helvetica Narrow Italic.

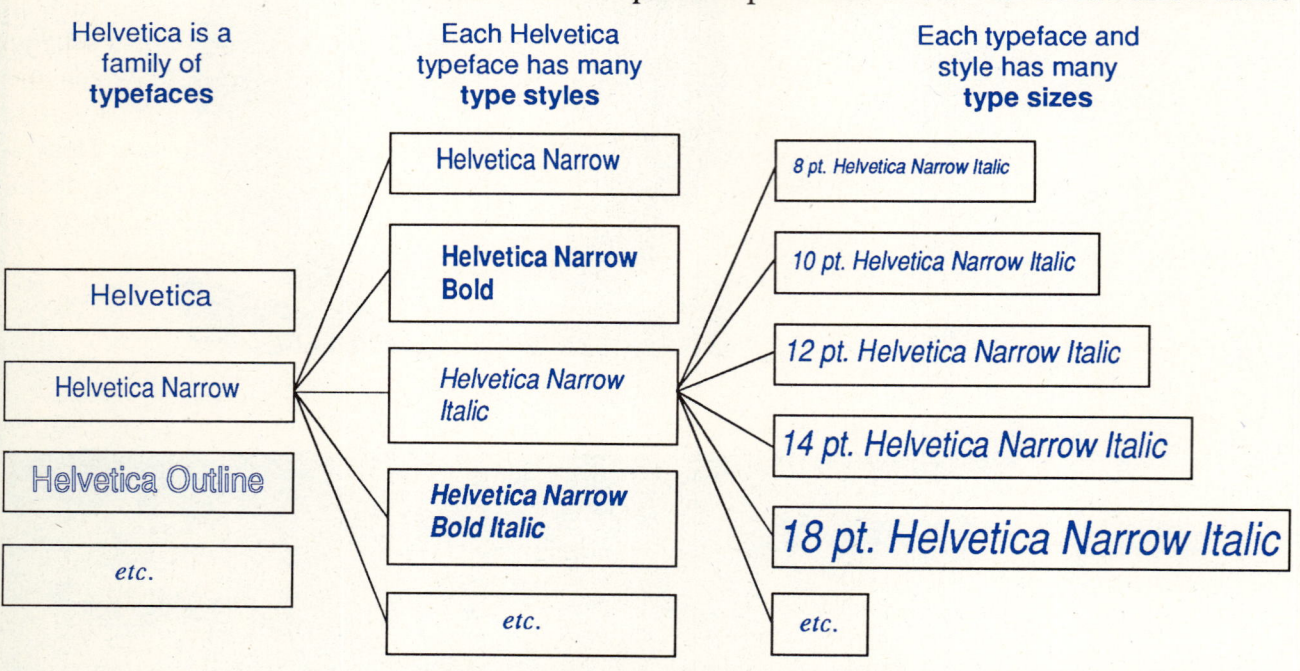

Helvetica is a family of **typefaces**
- Helvetica
- Helvetica Narrow
- Helvetica Outline
- etc.

Each Helvetica typeface has many **type styles**
- Helvetica Narrow
- **Helvetica Narrow Bold**
- Helvetica Narrow Italic
- **Helvetica Narrow Bold Italic**
- etc.

Each typeface and style has many **type sizes**
- 8 pt. Helvetica Narrow Italic
- 10 pt. Helvetica Narrow Italic
- 12 pt. Helvetica Narrow Italic
- 14 pt. Helvetica Narrow Italic
- 18 pt. Helvetica Narrow Italic
- etc.

H H

Schoolbook
Times Roman
Palatino
Courier

Helvetica is a **sans serif** typeface. That means it does not have any decorative lines or serifs at the ends of the letter strokes. New Century Schoolbook is a **serif** face. The word *serif* means "finishing stroke," like the finishing stroke on a letter written with a quill pen. The serifs help guide your eye to the next letter. Serif typefaces like New Century Schoolbook and Times Roman are easy to read in small sizes and are often used for text.

"As a rule," Rudi says, "we use serif faces like New Century Schoolbook, Times Roman, and Palatino for text because these faces are easy to read in smaller sizes. We use sans serif faces like Helvetica for headlines and captions because of their simple appearance. Sans serif faces are easy to read in large sizes."

Traditional serif faces are based on handwritten letters. The serif faces usually have letter strokes that vary in thickness. For example, the New Century Schoolbook letter *N* has vertical strokes that are much

Working with Typefaces

N N

thinner than the diagonal stroke. But there are some modern serif faces like Courier that break this tradition. Courier has serifs, but has strokes of the same thickness throughout. Courier was developed for IBM typewriters in 1952.

Rudi explains that type size is measured in points. She reminds you that one point is $1/72$ of an inch. For printing presses, type is cast in metal strips or blocks. The point size comes from measuring the height of the block holding the letters. Text is easy to read when it is 10 to 12 points in size. Special text, such as footnotes and captions, can be smaller. Heads and subheads can be printed in 18 or 14 point type, or you might use a 12 point boldface. Headlines and titles can be larger. Examine the titles and heads in this book for examples.

Spacing between lines of type can help make it more readable. Spacing between lines is called **leading**. This name comes from the thin strips of lead typesetters insert between lines of metal type to separate them. For example, two points of leading might be added between lines of 12 point type. Then each printed line will take 14 points of vertical space. Rudi says, "Typesetters call this setting type 12 on 14. Desktop publishing software has automatic leading. A common leading default is 12 on 14. It's easy to adjust the leading for more or less space between lines."

Type Leading:

This is a sample of 10 point Times Roman type printed with no leading (10 on 10). Times Roman is a typeface that was originally designed for use in the *London Times* newspaper.

This is a sample of 10 point Times Roman printed with 2 points of leading (10 on 12). The term *roman* is sometimes used to specify a vertical (not italic) type style.

This is a sample of 10 point Times Roman printed with 4 points of leading. The term *roman* has traditionally been used to mean an alternately thick and thin, serif typeface.

This is a sample of 12 point Times Roman printed with no leading (12 on 12). Times Roman is a typeface that was originally designed for use in the *London Times* newspaper.

This is a sample of 12 point Times Roman printed with 2 points of leading (12 on 14). The term *roman* is sometimes used to specify a vertical (not italic) type style.

This is a sample of 12 point Times Roman printed with 4 points of leading. The term *roman* has traditionally been used to mean an alternately thick and thin, serif typeface.

"Designing typefaces is an art," Rudi says. There are many famous typeface designers. Rudi's favorite is Hermann Zapf, who designed Palatino, a serif face, and Optima, a sans serif face. He also designed the Zapf Dingbats and Zapf Chancery, two popular special-purpose faces. Another famous designer is Stanley Morison, the creator of Times Roman. "If you like learning about type and enjoy using it," Rudi says, "you might want to become a type designer."

At one time, the designer planned a new typeface by making large, precise ink drawings of each character. Today, a special computer program can be used to design typefaces. The computer can calculate many variations of a font by changing characteristics such as the line thickness or height of the letters.

Stan points to an ornate typeface on Rudi's chart. "I would like to use this for a poster," he says. Rudi agrees, but says that Omega does not have this typeface on the laser printer. "Often customers want us to use a special font that we do not have on our printers," she explains. "I want you to help us show customers what typefaces they can select. For each of our printers, I'd like you to make a sample page that shows all the fonts that can be printed."

The second project Rudi has for you is to print samples of text using different faces, type sizes, and leading. The samples will help customers make selections for their publications. "Choosing type can be a complicated business. You must always specify the typeface, size, and style. You may need to specify the leading also. You must make certain the printer has the font it needs to print the type you have chosen."

Fill in the Work Assignment Log. Write the dates assigned and due dates for Chapter 5 work assignments. You will find the Work Assignment Log at the end of the chapter.

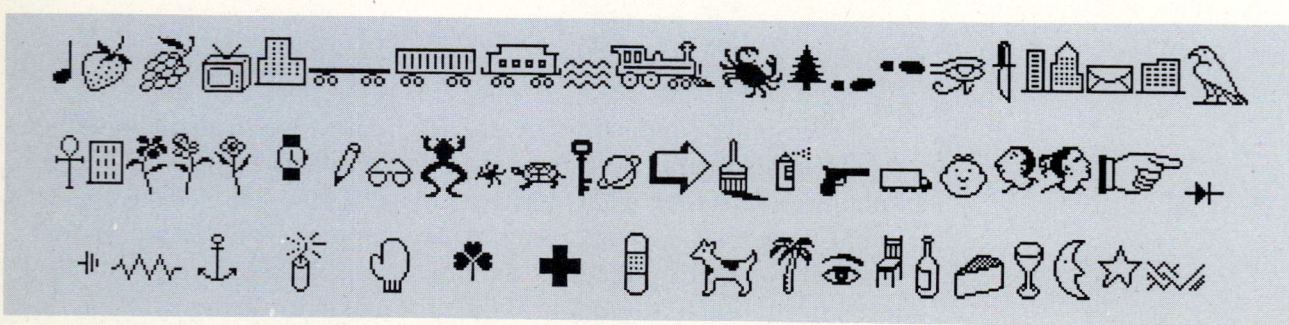

Two special fonts: Zapf Dingbats (top) and Cairo (bottom)

Name _____ Date _____ Period _____

SOFTWARE CHECK

✓ **Consult your software manual or guidesheet, watch a demonstration, and/or examine screen menus to answer these questions.**

What printers are available in your school lab? _____
_____
_____

How do you select the printer you will use for a publication? _____
_____
_____

What typefaces are available on the printers? _____
_____
_____

How do you select a typeface? _____
_____
_____

How do you specify the type size? _____
_____
_____

What type sizes can you select? _____
_____
_____

How do you specify the type style? _____
_____
_____

What type styles can you select? _____
_____
_____

How do you specify leading? _____
_____
_____

How do you specify two columns on a page? _____
_____
_____

FACT SHEET: INFORMATION ABOUT TYPEFACES

- Copyright laws do not apply to typefaces. Only the name of the typeface can be protected with a trademark. Fonts with names like *Helvetica* and *Times Roman* are not available on all printers. Often substitutes for these fonts are available that print almost identical faces. Substitutes for *Helvetica* are *Swiss*, *Helv*, and *Geneva*. Substitutes for *Times Roman* are *Dutch* and *New York*.

- **PostScript** is a special computer language called a "page description language." It tells laser printers that understand the PostScript language how to print the page. PostScript instructions tell the printer what face and style (font) to use, and the font size. The instructions also specify the position on the page and the characters to be printed. One advantage of the PostScript language is that it can tell the printer to scale (enlarge or reduce) a font to almost any point size. Other printers require a separate font for printing each size.

- Fonts are stored on computer disks as **screen fonts** and **printer fonts**. Screen fonts are displayed on the screen. Desktop publishing software tries to make the text on the screen look exactly like the printed text, but this is not always possible. If your printer prints with high resolution but your monitor cannot display in high resolution, the printed text will be much sharper than the text appears on the screen.

- Most typewriters have only **monospaced** typefaces. This means the same amount of space is used for every character. Most typefaces used in DTP are **proportionally spaced**. This means less space is used for narrow letters (*i*, *l*) than for wide letters (*m*, *w*). The same letters in different typefaces may vary in width. For example, Times Roman type takes less space than Palatino. In the same way, type sizes (height) vary slightly from one face to another.

AT THE EDITOR'S DESK

Leslie has explained that one area on which editors spend a lot of time is punctuation. Editors proofread text not only to make sure that the correct punctuation is used, but also to see that the correct number of spaces follow each punctuation mark.

Punctuation Mark	**Number of Spaces Following**
period at end of sentence	2
period after abbreviations (Mr. or No.)	1
period inside an abbreviation (C.O.D.)	0
period as a decimal point ($9.95)	0
comma	1
semicolon	1
colon	2
colon used in series of numbers (12:15)	0
quotation marks in body of sentence	1
quotation mark following the period at end of sentence	2
hyphen between words (brother-in-law)	0
hyphen when several words modify the same noun (one- or two-syllable word)	1, 0

To review the use of various punctuation marks, please study the Punctuation Guidelines in Appendix A. This will help you with your next editing assignments.

Here are two more proofreaders' marks for you to learn.

Proofreaders' Marks

≡ or (cap) Use either mark to show where capitals are needed, as in omega desktop, Inc.

○sp. Indicates an abbreviation should be spelled out. For example: DTP

Name _____ Date _____ Period _____

YOU, THE EDITOR!

PART 1   CORRECTING SPACING FOLLOWING PUNCTUATION MARKS

Instructions: Leslie has given you a letter that Mrs. Koyama wants to mail to a customer. He is satisfied with the way the letter sounds. However, he notices that the spacing following some punctuation marks as well as some of the punctuation is incorrect. Please proofread the letter and make the necessary corrections.

```
Ms.  Eleanor Lynch,  President
Wyndom Manufacturing,  Inc.
43325 Merion Way
Santa Rosa,  CA 95392

Dear Ms.  Lynch

Thank you for the opportunity to bid on your desktop
publishing project. We have examined your specification;  and
we offer the following cost breakdown for your review:

Keying text into computer             $500
Importing graphics                      50
Formatting text and graphics           350
Printing camera- ready copy             50
   Total Cost                         $950

If this price is acceptable to you,  we could start on the
project immediately. It will take approximately three days to
complete the work.

Sincerely yours



Aiko Koyama
President
```

PART 2   PROOFREADING FOR PUNCTUATION ERRORS

Instructions: Leslie has given you two more proofreading assignments with punctuation errors and with some missing punctuation. In addition, there are some long words that do not communicate as effectively as they should. Try to give shorter synonyms for these words. You may

83

reword sentences if you wish. Please make the necessary corrections on the following copy and then correct the disk file. If you are not using a template disk, key the information. If you are using a template disk, update the file ENERGY and print a copy.

```
              ENERGY AND THE ENVIRONMENT


    As everyone knows there has been a great deal of

discussion about our dwindling energy reserves.  Trying to

find new and inexpensive sources of energy as has exacerbated

some environmental problems.  The biggest problem of course

is disposing of nuclear waste.  There are also many toxic

waste dump sites across the country that are creating health

hazards.  Why in California alone toxic waste cleanup will

cost approximately four billion dollars--and every year

cleanup is postponed the cost increases.

    Air pollution caused by automobiles is also a problem.

We need to consider other sources of fuel that do not create

pollution.  solar power, wind power, ad battery power for

example.

    If you would like to join our discussion group to work

on these problems, you may do so by calling (787) 534-6892.

The Save the Environment Society would be happy to have you

join us on May 21 for a meeting.
```

PART 3 ADDITIONAL PROOFREADING FOR PUNCTUATION ERRORS

Instructions: This is a description of Omega's services that is to be printed in a new directory of businesses in a few weeks. Please edit and proofread the copy for punctuation errors.

```
Omega Desktop Inc
3245 Custer Street Santa Rosa
(787) 572- 7778

Store Hours :
Monday - Friday 7:00 a m - 9:00 p m
Saturday and Sunday 9:00 a m - 6:00 p m

Services:
Custom Layout and Desktop Publishing
Slef - Serve Macintosh and Laser Printing
Copying (same size, reductions and enlargements)
Typing Graphic Arts and Pasteup
Punching Collating and Stapling
Cutting and Special Handling
Binding (strip bind - self cover, paper, or vinyl covers)
```

Name _____ Date _____ Period _____

EXPLORING DESKTOP PUBLISHING

Complete the following activities to learn more about typefaces. In the activities, you will begin to build a collection of information about different typefaces. Share your collection with other class members so that everyone can have a complete set of type samples. By completing these activities and studying the results, you will learn to:

- Identify typefaces available to you.
- Recognize type styles for each typeface.
- Judge type set with different leading for readability.
- Determine the size of type.

DTP ACTIVITY 5A   PREPARING A TYPEFACE SAMPLE PAGE

Instructions: Complete the following steps to create a page showing the typefaces available on your printer. You will be making several copies of the same line to display the different typefaces.

1. Load the DTP software and open a new file called TYPESAMP. Set the page orientation to portrait. Use ¾ (.75) inch margins on all sides.
2. Select the printer you will be using for final output, if there is more than one printer available.
3. Enter the title, TYPEFACE SAMPLES PRINTED ON A *(printer name)*.
4. From the type menu, select the first typeface you will use. Select 12 points as the type size.
5. Enter the name of the typeface and the size. Then key the following line:

```
ABCDEFGHIJKLMNOPQRSTUVWXYZ   1234567890   abcdefghijklmnopqrstuvwxyz
```

6. Copy the line and insert it below the first line. Insert a copy for each type style you have available. If you have normal, italic, bold, and bold italic, you should insert three copies to have a total of four identical lines. After the last line, enter a blank line.
7. Make each line a different style. The first line should be normal. Select the other lines and change each to a different style. For example, make the second italic; the third, bold; and the fourth, bold italic.
8. Copy the block containing the typeface name, the four text lines, and the blank line for each typeface you have available.

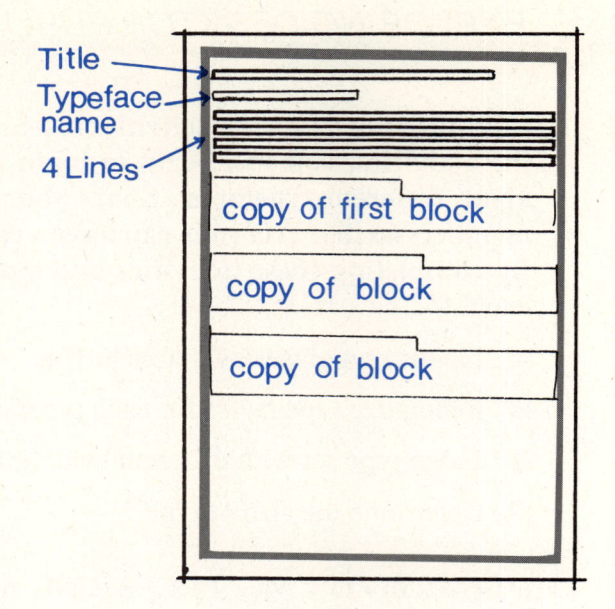

9. For each set of lines, change the typeface name on the first line to one of the typefaces available on your printer.
10. Select each set of lines and change the typeface to the face named in step 9. (Note: If necessary, repeat step 7 for each set.)
11. Save and print your sample page.

DTP ACTIVITY 5B   PREPARING A TYPE LEADING SAMPLE PAGE

Instructions: Select a typeface available on your printer. Then complete the following steps to create a page showing different leading for three sizes of the typeface.

1. Open a file and name it TYPELEAD. Set the page orientation to portrait. Use one column, with 2½ (2.5) inch margins on each side and ¾ (.75) inch margins at the top and bottom.
2. Key the name of the typeface you have chosen at the top of the column. Select the name and set it in the typeface you have selected using 14 point bold as the size and style.
3. Key a paragraph. Key the first sentence: "This is a sample of 8 point *(typeface name)* printed with no leading (8 on 8 or 8/8)." Continue with other information about the typeface. Key at least four lines. Copy from these lines if there is not enough information about the typeface to fill four lines. Enter a blank line at the end of the paragraph.
4. Select the paragraph and the blank line. Set the typeface to the one you have chosen. Set the type size to 8 points. Set the leading to 8

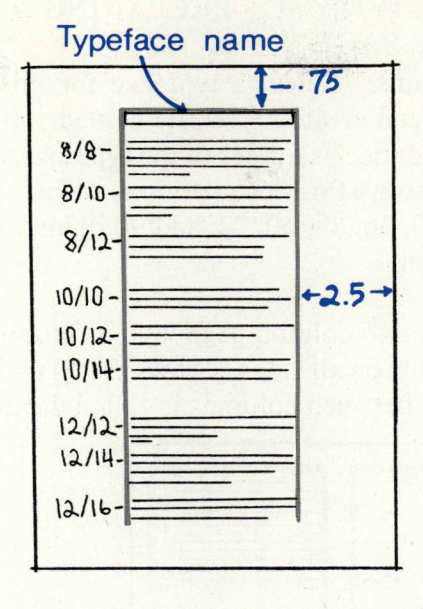

Typeface name [diagram with measurements: ←.75 at top, ←2.5→ width, rows labeled 8/8, 8/10, 8/12, 10/10, 10/12, 10/14, 12/12, 12/14, 12/16]

points. Copy the paragraph and blank line. Insert two copies, so that you have a total of three paragraphs.

5. Change the first sentence of the second paragraph to read: "This is a sample of 8 point *(typeface name)* printed with 2 points leading (8 on 10 or 8/10)." Select the paragraph and change the leading to 10 points.
6. Change the first sentence of the third paragraph to read: "This is a sample of 8 point *(typeface name)* printed with 4 points leading (8 on 12 or 8/12)." Select the paragraph and change the leading to 12 points.
7. Enter a blank line after the third paragraph.
8. Copy the three paragraphs and the blank line. Insert two copies after the blank line. Now you will have three sets of three paragraphs each.
9. Select the second set and change the type size for all paragraphs to 10 points. Set the leading in the first paragraph to no leading (10 on 10); in the second, to 2 points leading (10 on 12), and in the third, to 4 points leading (10 on 14). Change the text in each paragraph to show the settings you used for it.
10. In the third set, change the type size for all paragraphs to 12 points. Set the leading in the paragraphs to no leading (12 on 12), 2 points leading (12 on 14), and 4 points leading (12 on 16). Change the text in each paragraph to show the settings you used for it.
11. If the sample paragraphs will not fit in one column, delete the last line in each paragraph of the third set.
12. Print your sample page. Mark the paragraphs that seem most readable to you.
13. Exchange copies of your results for copies of results from other students who used other typefaces.

DTP ACTIVITY 5C   PREPARING A TYPE SIZE AND STYLE SAMPLE PAGE

Instructions: Select a typeface for this activity. Load your DTP software and create a new file named TYPESIZE. Then follow the steps listed to produce samples of the type sizes available on your printer. If you are using a PostScript printer, make samples for 6, 8, 10, 12, 14, 16, 18, 24, 30, 36, 48, 60, 72, and 90 point type. Remember to save your work often.

1. Use a two-column page layout for this activity. Use ³/₄ (.75) inch margins on all sides. Leave ¹/₂ (.5) inch between the columns. The space between columns is called the **gutter**.

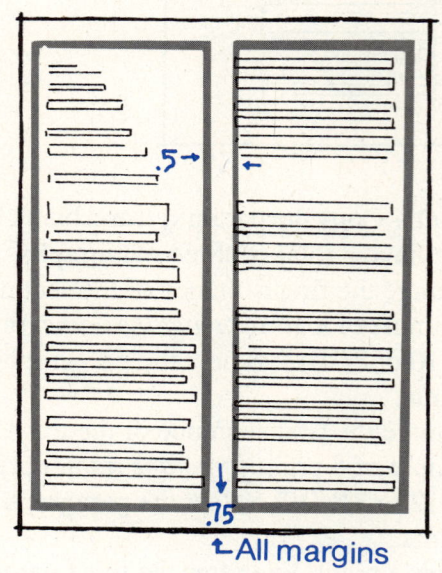

2. At the top of the first column, enter the heading SIZES AND STYLES—*(typeface name)*. Set this heading in the typeface you have chosen using 14 point bold.

3. Enter these lines:

```
6 pt. (typeface name) Normal
6 pt. (typeface name) Italic
6 pt. (typeface name) Bold
6 pt. (typeface name) Bold Italic
```
(blank line)

4. Select each line and set the type style to match the style indicated in the line.

5. Copy the four text lines and the blank line. Insert a copy for each type size that you have available from 6 through 36 points. You may have up to ten sets of the five lines. Use both columns, if necessary.

6. Select the second set of lines and change the type size to the next larger size, such as 8 point. Change each line to indicate the point size.
7. Repeat step 6 for each set of lines that you inserted in step 5, increasing the type size each time, until you reach 36 point, or the largest size available on your printer.
8. If you are using a printer that can print type larger than 36 point, you may be able to create samples of 48, 60, 72, and 90 point type. For these sizes, enter the point size and as much of the typeface name as will fit on one line in the column. Use the normal style only. Select the line and set the typeface and size.
9. When the sample page is complete, first save your publication and then print a copy. If possible, make photocopies of your page for the other students in your class. Exchange copies of your type size sampler with classmates who used other typefaces.

Name _____ Date _____ Period _____

VOCABULARY REVIEW

vo·cab·u·lary

The following terms are used in Chapter 5 and are defined in the Glossary. Match the definitions to the terms by placing the letter of the correct definition in the space provided. Review Chapter 5 or the Glossary for any terms you do not remember. Not all definitions will be used.

Terms	Definitions
____ 1. typeface	A. variations of a typeface, such as bold
____ 2. type style	B. a set of type of one face, style, and size
____ 3. gutter	C. spacing between lines of type
____ 4. italic	D. letter strokes end in decorative lines
____ 5. font	E. used to measure type
____ 6. serif	F. a page description language
____ 7. sans serif	G. all letters use the same amount of space
____ 8. leading	H. a set of type with the same design
____ 9. PostScript	I. a type style with slanting letters
____ 10. monospaced	J. without decorative lines at the end of the letter strokes
	K. the space between columns

TREASURE HUNT

Collect examples of at least five different layouts that you like. Look for one-column, two-column, and three-column layouts. Find a layout that uses two facing pages. Try to determine:

- What fonts are used? Use the samples you printed to help identify the typefaces, styles, and sizes.

- How wide are the columns? How many characters are there per line?

- How much leading is used? Rate the readability of each example on a scale of 1 to 5, with 5 high.

- Note where titles and captions are placed and how photos and drawings are combined with the text. Is there any empty space in the layout? Where is the white space? Do you think it helps the layout?

WORK ASSIGNMENT LOG

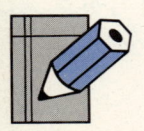

Fill in the "Date Assigned" and "Date Due" columns for each assignment that your teacher makes. When you complete an assignment, enter the date in the "Date Completed" column.

Chapter 5 Work Assignments	Date Assigned	Date Due	Date Completed
Software Check			
You, the Editor! Part 1			
You, the Editor! Part 2			
You, the Editor! Part 3			
DTP Activity 5A			
DTP Activity 5B			
DTP Activity 5C			
Vocabulary Review			
Treasure Hunt			

Turn in Chapter 5 assignments after you have completed all of them, or follow your teacher's instructions. When these assignments are returned to you, put them in your publishing handbook.

CHAPTER 6
COMMUNICATING
THROUGH PAGE LAYOUT

CHAPTER OBJECTIVES

When you have completed this chapter, you will be able to:

- ✓ Use a page grid to organize page layout.
- ✓ Recognize symmetrical and asymmetrical layouts.
- ✓ Use variety and contrast in page design.
- ✓ Use visual elements to communicate information.
- ✓ Edit for grammatical errors.

INTRODUCTION

Rudi calls you and Stan into her office. Leslie is there working at Rudi's desk. There are sheets of paper scattered on Rudi's drawing table and pinned on the wall above it. Leslie is studying a page of thumbnail sketches.

Rudi explains to you and Stan, "I have been sketching layouts for a brochure of page design tips for our customers. Leslie and I wrote the copy for the brochure. We want to use the tips in the brochure design. Then the brochure will illustrate the tips. Can you help us decide on a layout?"

Leslie agrees that the layout should help communicate what he and Rudi have written. He hands you the copy to read. The first part describes the **page grid**. The page grid establishes the margins and columns for a page. It is the first thing you would draw in a thumbnail sketch. The page grid should be the same for every page in a publication. This will give the publication a unified appearance. Some desktop publishing software lets you create **master pages** with the page grid on them. The software copies the measurements you set for margins and columns in the master pages to each page in the publication.

There can be one or several columns on a page. The best width for a column depends upon the size of the type used. Rudi has included the following chart to give the preferred column widths for different sizes of type. The chart gives the type sizes in points and the column widths in picas.

Recommended Column Widths

TYPE SIZE:	6	8	10	12	14
Minimum Length (picas)	8	9	13	14	18
Optimum Length (picas)	10	13	16	21	24
Maximum Length (picas)	12	16	20	24	28

Source: *Font & Function*, The Adobe Type Catalog, Spring/1989

Rudi shows you two thumbnail sketches for the brochure. One has two columns of the same width on the page. There is a vertical line, called a **rule**, between the columns. "This layout is **symmetrical**," she says. Both sides of the page are the same. It has a balanced appearance. Everything on the page seems to be in the right place.

The second sketch has two columns, but the one on the right is wider than the other. This layout is **asymmetrical**. Rudi has sketched several

Communicating Through Page Layout

heads in bold type in the narrow left column. The heads help balance the text in the right column. Rudi plans to place a graphic in the left column also. Everything on this page seems to be in the right place too, but this layout seems more interesting than the first one.

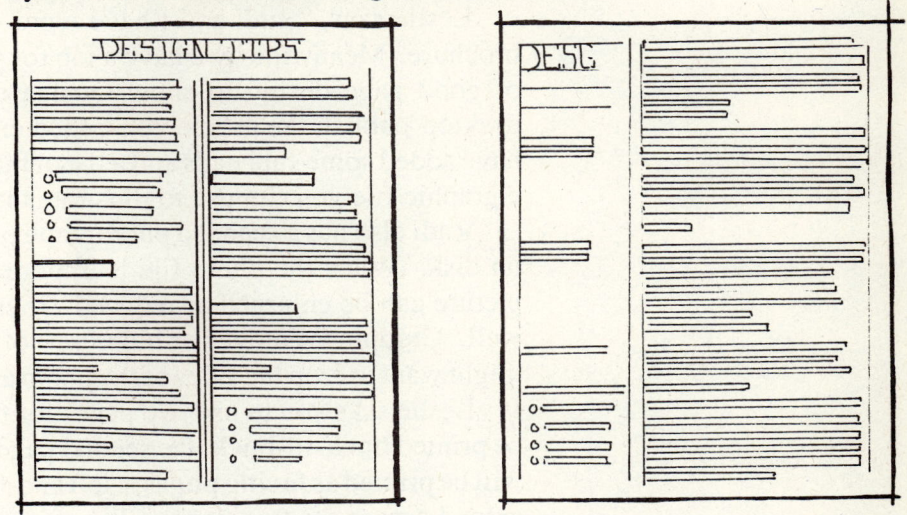

The brochure copy explains that good page design will attract the reader. Designers use different tools to make the page interesting. One of these is variety. The asymmetrical page has more variety than the symmetrical page.

Rudi thinks that designers must be careful not to have too much variety in their page layouts. If too many typefaces, illustrations, heads, and blocks of text are combined on a page, the page will be too busy. "Try to find a happy medium between busy and boring," Rudi says.

There is a section in the design tips brochure about choosing type for a publication. Usually no more than two typefaces are needed. By choosing a serif face and a sans serif face, you can have variety and create an interesting contrast in type design. Contrast is another way to attract the reader's attention.

The tips say that you can use white space to create contrast and attract the attention of the reader. White space contrasts with the gray tones of the printed areas. White space gives the eye a place to rest. A page with areas of white space is more inviting to read than a page filled solidly with type.

There are several lists in the brochure copy. Rudi plans to set these as **bullet lists**. Bullet lists have a special character ahead of each item, like the Chapter Objectives and Fact Sheets in this book. Rudi explains that when the lists are set off with bullets, the reader can recognize them at once as lists of items. In the same way, using the same typeface and style for subheads helps the reader tell which heads have equal importance.

"Consistency in page design is very important to readers," Rudi says. By using type and other visual elements in the same way every time, you can help the reader see quickly how the different parts of the page are related. Visual elements like rules, bullets, and the position of heads and illustrations can communicate information about the page contents. With consistent use of good page design, you can help the reader understand the printed information.

Leslie says, "Rudi and I have more work to do on the design tips brochure. Meanwhile, we have a job for you. We need some examples of good page design to show Omega customers. We want you to desktop-publish the article you edited entitled 'The King of Rock.' I have added some subheads and a list of hit albums by Stevens. Rudi has a graphic file you can use to illustrate the article."

Rudi also has a scanned photograph of Stevens. The photo is stored on disk. When the photo file is imported into the DTP software, the picture can be enlarged or reduced. It can be **cropped** or trimmed as well. Cropping removes or hides part of the photo. For example, you might want to crop the sides of the photo and use only the center portion.

Leslie asks you to use two pages for the article. The pages will not be printed **back-to-back,** the second page on the back of the first. They will be printed as **facing pages,** a left and a right page. The layout should extend across the two pages. Two facing pages that are planned as a single layout are called a **double spread**. Try to follow the design tips to make the pages attractive to the reader.

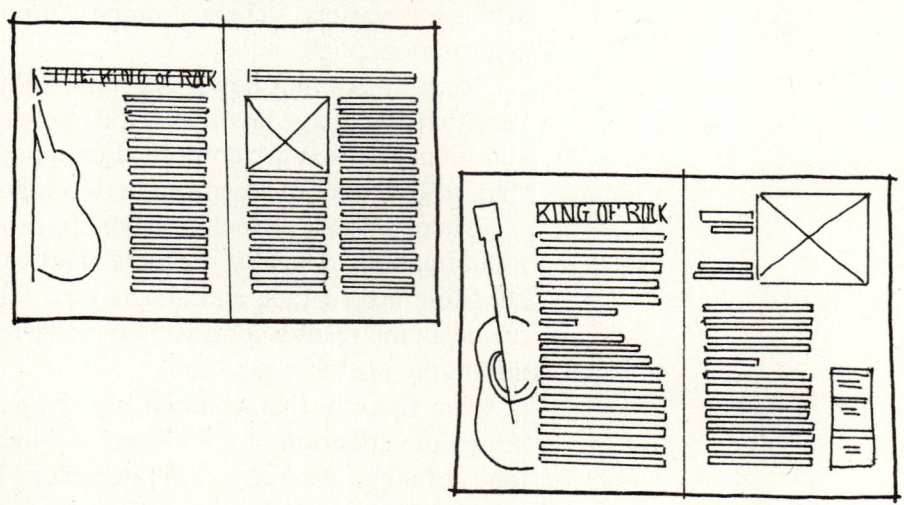

Fill in the Work Assignment Log. Write the dates assigned and due dates for Chapter 6 work assignments. You will find the Work Assignment Log at the end of the chapter.

Name _____ Date _____ Period _____

SOFTWARE CHECK

Can you perform the following operations with your DTP software? If so, what menu or method do you use? Check your software manual or the information sheet your teacher gives you.

How do you create a page grid? _____
_____
_____

How do you create master pages? _____
_____
_____

How do you change the width of columns? _____
_____
_____

How do you create rules between columns? _____
_____
_____

How do you view facing pages? _____
_____
_____

How do you create bullets? _____
_____
_____

How do you use special characters for bullets? _____
_____
_____

How do you import scanned photographs? _____
_____
_____

FACT SHEET: PAGE LAYOUT CONSIDERATIONS

- When readers browse through a bound publication, like a magazine or book, they often hold it by the binding. As they flip the pages, they may see just the outside half of each page. To attract their attention, use an eye-catching design element in the outside half of the page.

- If pages are to be bound, leave extra space in the margin on the side where the page will be bound. If a double spread will be folded, and not bound, leave less space in the margin on the fold side. Some DTP software packages will automatically **mirror** left and right page layouts. They will put the wider margin on the opposite side for the left and right pages, as if you were viewing the page in a mirror.

- Very large type, called **display type**, is sometimes used as a graphic element in page design. Words set in display type communicate not only their meaning but also visually by their position and appearance.

- Some elements that can be contrasted in a layout are:

text	☐	white space
text	☐	pictures
small text	☐	large text
small heads	☐	display type
vertical lines	☐	horizontal lines
vertical shapes	☐	horizontal shapes
empty spaces	☐	full spaces
regular arrangements	☐	irregular arrangements

- Standard page layouts for specific documents can be created by saving page grids as **templates**. Templates are available for newsletters, brochures, reports, and many other documents. Customized templates may have special features such as logos, page numbers, rules, and other graphic elements that are used in the document.

AT THE EDITOR'S DESK

Editors must be alert for grammatical errors. Some of the most common errors include the following:

Agreement Between Subject and Verb

The verb must always agree with its subject in number. Words that mean "one" (*woman*, *man*, *tree*, *dog*) are singular; words that mean "more than one" (*women*, *men*, *trees*, *dogs*) are plural. If the subject is singular, the verb that goes with it must be singular; if the subject is plural, the verb that goes with it must be plural.

Wrong:

Three months of my work was wasted.

Right:

Three months of my work were wasted.

Wrong:

One of the dogs bite children.

Right:

One of the dogs bites children.

Dangling Modifiers

Modifiers are words or phrases that add to the meaning of other sentence elements by describing them. Modifiers "dangle" when there is no word to which they can clearly relate.

Wrong:

Our vacation passed happily, swimming and playing volleyball.

Right:

We passed our vacation happily, swimming and playing volleyball.

Wrong:

After seeing the dentist, her teeth stopped aching.
(Her teeth did not see the dentist; she did.)

Right:

After she saw the dentist, her teeth stopped aching.

Parallelism

Parallelism in grammar refers to sentence elements that closely correspond to each other. Parallel sentence elements linked by coordinating conjunctions (*and*, *but*, *or*, etc.) must be parallel in form. Noun must parallel noun, adjective must parallel adjective, verb must parallel verb, etc.

Wrong:

A good scholar must be precise and possess patience.

Right:

A good scholar must be precise and patient.

Wrong:

Give me a bright woman who has initiative.

Right:

Give me a woman who is bright and has initiative.

Wrong:

Saturday I went to a movie, shopping at the supermarket, and had dinner at El Tecolete Restaurant.

Right:

Saturday I went to a movie, shopped at the supermarket, and had dinner at El Tecolete Restaurant.

Here are two more proofreaders' marks to use in your editing assignments.

Proofreaders' Marks

___   A line under a word means to underline.

¶   This mark at the beginning of a sentence means "start a new paragraph." ¶ Always start a paragraph on a new line.

Name _____ Date _____ Period _____

YOU, THE EDITOR!

Complete the following exercises to give you practice editing copy for grammatical errors. When you finish, write the date in the "Date Completed" column of your Work Assignment Log.

PART 1 CORRECTING DANGLING MODIFIERS

Instructions: Rewrite the following sentences so the modifiers are in the proper position.

1. Columbus vowed as soon as he landed to claim the New World for Ferdinand and Isabella.
2. He promised to visit us as we were leaving.
3. Because food spoils when not in use it should always be refrigerated.
4. Hanging from the top of the building, crowds watched as the fanatic prepared to leap.
5. Working too hard and earning too little, my nervousness increased.
6. Before leaving for Canada, reservations must be made.
7. When entering the theater, the noise made by the audience surprised me.
8. I only told the jury what I had seen.

PART 2 EDITING TO CORRECT GRAMMAR

Instructions: A customer has brought in a page of telephone techniques to be edited. Please make the necessary corrections so subjects and verbs agree, dangling modifiers are eliminated, and all sentences have parallel structure. Watch for misspelled words, missing punctuation, and unnecessary words. Indicate where type might be underlined or made bold.

TELEPHONE TECHNIQUES

   The telephone is often your only link to people outside the office. The use of your voice is vital in communicating emotions, courtesy, and in transmitting the intent of your message. The person is unable to draw conclusions at the other end from your physical manner and body gestures. The

---

Continued

caller is unable to see your smile or the concern in your eyes so that your voice over the telephone must be the sole vehicle of effective communication. Your personality needs to shine through.

Be alert. You should always answer the telephone promptly. If you are already on a line, put the caller on hold by courteously saying, "Could you hold a minute please? I have another incoming call. Answer the ringing line as follows: "Good afternoon, Clark and Grindall. Could you hold a moment?"

You then place the second called on hold and return to your first call. Do not allow more than two calls to remain on hold if they are personally waiting for you. Ask if you can return the call, taking the telephone number and name of the caller, and return the call as soon as your other calls are cleared. If the caller wishes to be connected to another person, switch him or her directly, or offer to take a message.

Be pleasant. Put a smile on your face; pleasantness is said to be contagious. If you are able to transmit a cheerful attitude to callers, their responses are likely to be cheerful too.

Continued

Be natural. Use simple language. Avoid slang terms. Do not use mechanical robot-like phrases. Try to treat each call as if it is the only call of the day. This is not always easy especially as the day progresses and people grow more irritable, but try!

Speak distinctly. Speak clearly, not mumbling, and speak directly into the transmitter. Speak in a moderate tone of voice. Speak loud enough for the caller to hear you, but not so loud as to disturb other people in the office around you.

Be expressive. A well-modulated voice carries best over the telephone. Keep an even pace. Do not talk excessively fast or excessively slow. By varying the pitch of your voice, you can add emphasis and make your conversation more interesting which will help to present the true intent of your words and will add vitality to your speech.

Name   Date   Period

EXPLORING DESKTOP PUBLISHING

Complete the DTP activities. When you finish each activity, write the date in the "Date Completed" column of your Work Assignment Log. By completing these activities, you will learn how to:

- Study page layouts and analyze their design.
- Plan a double spread using text files and illustrations.
- Desktop-publish the double spread.

DTP ACTIVITY 6A   ANALYZING PAGE LAYOUTS

Instructions: Make thumbnail sketches of two of the page layouts that you collected for the Chapter 5 Treasure Hunt. Look for these features and note them on your sketches:

- Visual elements that organize the page and help the reader.
- The size of margins and other areas of white space.
- How the page is divided into columns.
- The placement of blocks of text.
- The placement of graphic elements, such as rules and display type.
- The placement of the page number.
- The use of illustrations.
- The use of white space.
- The consistent (or inconsistent) use of heads or other page elements.
- Other special features on the page.

DTP ACTIVITY 6B   CREATING THE "KING OF ROCK" PUBLICATION

Instructions: The edited copy for the "King of Rock" article follows. The scanned photo and graphic are also shown. The article is in the file KINGROC2 on your template disk. Plan to include the list of hit albums from the file ROCKHITS. The scanned photograph file is called STEVENS. The graphic file is named GUITAR. If you are not using a template disk, use your KINGROCK file from Chapter 3. These are the steps you should follow:

1. Read the "King of Rock" article again and plan how you will set the title and heads. Plan the locations of illustrations. Plan the type size and leading. Remember, you can use display type as a graphic element. You can use bullets to set off lists.
2. Make at least three thumbnail sketches of page layouts for the two facing pages. The double spread will be bound in the center. Select

the layout you think will work best. You might ask others for their opinions and suggestions.
3. Create the two pages with your DTP software. If necessary, modify your layout when you see it at full size. You may need to resize or crop the illustrations to match your layout. If you cannot import the scanned photo with your DTP software, manually paste up the copy of the photo from Appendix B.
4. Save your file and name it KINGROC3.
5. Print a proof copy and adjust your layout in the DTP software or with manual pasteup.

THE KING OF ROCK IS BACK--WITH NEW PRIORITIES

Santa Rosa--George Stevens made his reputation over ten years ago with high voltage performances that turned his downbeat songs about despair and death into upbeat, life-affirming songs of joy. Few performers have ever exhibited such intensity and desire.

But this morning, the king of rock in the late '70s and early '80s is tiptoeing back and forth down the hall of a comfortable hotel checking on his children who are sleeping in another room. His wife is out shopping.

The rock star, now 43, has just reentered the pop world after taking a six-year break. During that time, he married, moved to Scotland (the birthplace of his wife), and started raising a family. George Stevens has a new set of priorities. He wants to perform, but he also wants to enjoy his roles as husband and father. He interrupts the interview several times to check on Matthew, 4, and Erin, 2.

Continued

Though Stevens misses the States, he plans to continue living in Scotland with his wife, Maraise Evans--a well-known artist--and their two children. They are both very pleased about the third child they expect to arrive in three months. Stevens says he will continue to make albums, write songs, and make occasional personal appearances, but he won't tour.

Won't tour? Sacrilege! Is this the same man who, after breaking his leg in a 1980 fall from a stage platform, did his act in a full leg cast? In reflecting on his fall, he says: "I just couldn't hold back. There was a moment when I felt I could fly and I just soared off the platform. It was a six-foot drop and I didn't land properly. I was aware of the danger. I had never tried the jump before. But something inside me just pushed me over."

New Priorities

Asked about the differences between the old George Stevens and the new one, he explains, "When you are young and single and a rock star, you have the luxury of being romantic about life and death. You can be frivolous. When you have a loving partner and children, you have a responsibility to take care of yourself. You have to spend time with them.

Continued

Children depend on you for everything. You can't be daydreaming about exploding like a fireball on stage. You have new priorities."

Stevens is one of several celebrated pop stars to take a sabbatical. Some of the breaks from the fast lane have been the result of legal or physical problems, but the tendency seems to be toward a voluntary respite. The trend is likely to gain momentum as veteran artists see the time away from tours as a means of revitalizing their art.

About his own decision to step away from the pop music world, Stevens says, "When you are on tour all the time, your life becomes a big swirl. Relationships with those you love become too intense or else lose all sense of intimate communication. You don't have time to step back and put everything in perspective."

The Maturing of Rock

Sabbaticals are a sign of the maturing of rock. Recording stars used to be under tremendous pressure to keep turning out new singles and keep touring because rock music was considered a fad.

Continued

Things are different now. Rock has become a multibillion-dollar-a-year institution. Performers are telling recording companies when to expect new releases rather than delivering them on a company timetable. Artists now think in terms of long careers. The thought of taking time off is no longer seen as "bad for business." In some cases, it makes good sense.

Stevens's case is especially interesting because his break was open-ended. He walked away without any promise to return. When asked if he has any regrets, George replies, "Regrets are futile--but no, I have none. It was right for me to walk away then just as it is right for me to be active again now. I feel stronger and healthier because of the break. I think my music is better than it was five years ago."

The fans certainly seem to agree. They gave Stevens continuous standing ovations for more than half his show at his first series of comeback performances. Welcome back George! We've missed you!

Continued

```
George Stevens's hits of the '70s:

George Stevens and the Green Street Band:  Live 1978-80
Dreams of Love and Life
Memories of Better Times
Between Us
Sugar Candy
Live Coals and Hot Rocks
```

George Stevens in Central Park, 1981

Name _____ Date _____ Period _____

VOCABULARY REVIEW

vo-cab-u-lary

The following terms are used in Chapter 6 and are defined in the Glossary. Match the definitions to the terms by placing the letter of the correct definition in the space provided. Review Chapter 6 or the Glossary for any terms you do not remember. Not all definitions will be used.

Terms

_____ 1. page grid
_____ 2. modifier
_____ 3. asymmetrical
_____ 4. mirror
_____ 5. bullet list
_____ 6. display type
_____ 7. crop
_____ 8. double spread
_____ 9. template
_____ 10. rule

Definitions

A. a page grid saved and used as a pattern
B. to trim an illustration
C. the two sides are the same
D. very large type used as a graphic element
E. layout of margins and columns
F. items set off by a special character
G. the two sides are different
H. a line between columns
I. layout extends across facing pages
J. left page grid is reversed for right page
K. adds to the meaning of other words

TREASURE HUNT

To continue your study of page design and layout, collect examples of posters and advertisements that use graphics. Try to find unusual arrangements of graphics and type that appeal to you. Look in computer magazines for samples that might have been created on a computer. Look for these types of graphics:

- Display type used as a graphic element.
- Text charts that are mostly words and numbers.
- Statistical graphs that represent numbers as lines or icons and symbols.
- Maps and engineering diagrams.
- Cartoons and realistic drawings.
- Photographs.

WORK ASSIGNMENT LOG

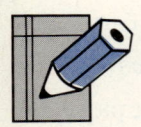

Fill in the "Date Assigned" and "Date Due" columns for each assignment that your teacher makes. When you complete an assignment, enter the date in the "Date Completed" column.

Chapter 6 Work Assignments	Date Assigned	Date Due	Date Completed
Software Check			
You, the Editor! Part 1			
You, the Editor! Part 2			
DTP Activity 6A			
DTP Activity 6B			
Vocabulary Review			
Treasure Hunt			

Turn in Chapter 6 assignments after you have completed all of them, or follow your teacher's instructions. When these assignments are returned to you, put them in your publishing handbook.

CHAPTER 7
USING GRAPHICS
IN DESKTOP PUBLISHING

CHAPTER OBJECTIVES

When you have completed this chapter, you will be able to:

- ✔ Use DTP graphic tools to enhance the layout.
- ✔ Select and arrange graphics to support the text.
- ✔ Recognize different types of graphic files.
- ✔ Write effective opening sentences.
- ✔ Write effective paragraphs.

INTRODUCTION

After several weeks of working at Omega Desktop, Inc., your favorite job is helping customers produce the documents they need. You are especially pleased to show them how to use the DTP software to make professional-looking pages. Lately there has been a demand for posters and brochures. Rudi asks you for help in preparing poster layouts.

"We need to design some standard layouts that our customers can use for their posters. They will be made up like templates. Each one should use graphics to help attract attention to the poster and to the information in it." Rudi explains that posters are like other DTP products, except that large display type is used and illustrations or other graphics are usually in the poster. Designing a poster layout will help you learn more about using graphics, Rudi explains.

First you need to know about the kinds of graphics your DTP software can create. Then you must learn to recognize the two different kinds of graphic files the DTP software can import.

Rudi demonstrates some of the drawing tools in the DTP software. On a blank screen, she quickly draws a few lines with the **freehand tool**. With the freehand tool, it is possible to draw curved or straight lines in any direction, in much the same way that you would draw with a pencil and no mechanical aids. Rudi selects other tools and uses them to draw exact straight lines and boxes. She demonstrates how to move the boxes, how to fill boxes with a pattern, and how to erase them. **Fill patterns** are dots, lines, or colors used within a shape.

Rudi draws a rectangle and makes a copy of it. Then she makes one of the rectangles black and moves it behind the other rectangle to make a **shadow box**. "A shadow box is a good way to get attention," she explains.

SHADOW BOX

Next Rudi chooses the text tool. She types the word *reverse*. She shows how to change the letters to white type on a black background. This is called a **reverse** because the letters are white on a black background instead of black on a white background. Reverses are another way to get attention.

REVERSE

"This next tool is my favorite," Rudi says. She selects another tool and draws a box with round corners. She shows how to make the box outline thicker. Rudi explains that before there were computers to draw this shape, graphic artists had to draw the arcs at each corner very carefully so the arcs would match the lines on the sides perfectly. This tedious job took a long time. With the computer, Rudi can do the same thing in a few seconds.

Omega has several graphic programs and a scanner. Omega has the two types of graphic programs: **paint programs** and **draw programs**. Rudi shows you examples of graphics she has made with a paint program. Paint programs make bit-mapped graphics. A **bit-mapped graphic** shows a record of each tiny dot or **pixel** of the computer screen and whether the pixel is turned off or turned on. If the computer screen resolution is 72 pixels per inch, there will be a record of 72 x 72 pixels for each square inch. That is over 5,000 pixels! When you look closely at the paint graphic, you can see the tiny dots that make up the picture. A graphic made with the scanner also has the tiny dots. It is bit-mapped too.

Rudi has a picture of a school bus. It looks much sharper than the bit-mapped pictures. It was made with a draw program and printed on the laser printer. Rudi explains that draw programs do not use a bit-map. Instead, draw programs make files that have instructions for drawing the objects. The instructions might say, "Go to this point on the screen. Draw a line that goes to this point. Make the line this thick." Because draw program instructions are for drawing objects, graphics created with draw programs are called **object-oriented graphics**. When the instructions are sent to a laser printer, it can print the objects using 300 dots per inch. This makes sharper lines than bit-mapped lines.

There are other software programs Rudi uses for graphics. Most of these programs are used to change picture files so that they can be imported into the DTP software. For example, not all DTP software can use files made with draw programs. Rudi can use the special software to change the files into bit-mapped files that the DTP software can use.

Fill in the Work Assignment Log. Write the dates assigned and due dates for Chapter 7 work assignments. You will find the Work Assignment Log at the end of the chapter.

Name _____ Date _____ Period _____

SOFTWARE CHECK

Read the Fact Sheet, consult your software manual or guidesheet, watch a demonstration, and/or examine screen menus for information to answer the following questions.

List the drawing tools available with your DTP software: _____
_____
_____

Can you perform the following operations with your DTP software? If so, what menu or method do you use?

How do you change line weights? _____
_____
_____

How do you choose fill patterns? _____
_____
_____

How do you import bit-mapped graphics? _____
_____
_____

File formats: _____
How do you create and edit bit-mapped graphics? _____
_____
_____

How do you import object-oriented graphics? _____
_____
_____

File formats: _____
How do you crop graphic images? _____
_____
_____

How do you size graphic images? _____
_____
_____

FACT SHEET: USING GRAPHIC IMAGES

- Pages with bit-mapped graphic images on them will take longer to print than pages with only text. The bit-mapped files are large because they contain information about every pixel. Because of the size of these files, they take longer to print. To save time printing proof copies, spend more time planning your layout with sketches. Then cut up your first proof copy to experiment with layout changes before you revise and print again.

- Different graphic programs store files in different formats. You must know which file formats your DTP software can use. Different computers also use different graphic file formats. If you are using a template disk, you will discover that the files were prepared for the DTP software and the computer you are using. You may be able to convert other graphic files into a format your DTP software can use with special **file conversion software.**

- Many of the graphic files on the template disk are scanned images. They were made from photographs and drawings and stored as bit-mapped files. You may have noticed that they are black and white, with no shades of gray. Photographs can be stored as **gray-mapped** files. Then the shades of gray in the photographs will be reproduced. Gray-mapped files are very large. One file might take an entire disk or more.

- Another kind of software that is often useful for creating graphic files is called **screen capture software.** These programs will take a picture of the computer screen and save it as a bit-mapped file. For example, you might display a graphic on the screen and take its picture. You can edit the file with a paint program or with the DTP software, if the DTP software can edit graphics.

AT THE EDITOR'S DESK

Leslie says, "You're doing great! You've developed some good editing skills and you are becoming a valuable asset to the firm." Here are some more editing tips for you to practice.

One of the most important concepts in effective writing is the paragraph. A paragraph provides the organizational structure for an article or story. A paragraph should consist of one topic sentence and several supporting sentences. The length of the paragraph depends on the purpose of the writer and the needs of the reader. In technical writing or complicated instructions, paragraphs should be short. This helps the reader cope with the material. Newspapers and magazines use paragraphs of one or two sentences to keep the reader's attention. In novels and essays, a paragraph might be 200 to 300 words long.

The length of the paragraph is not as important as how completely the paragraph makes its point. If the topic sentence is flabby, containing unnecessary words, the supporting sentences tend to be less than precise. If the writing provides the bare minimum of detail, the reader is left wanting more information.

Remember, paragraphs give you control. They help you to make writing more concise and keep you from straying from the point.

The topic sentence is usually the opening sentence of the paragraph. This is not always so, but it is a good way to organize material until you become more skilled. Without a good opening sentence, the writer struggles to shape the paragraph and the reader struggles to understand it. The paragraph's first sentence should tell the reader what to expect. The remaining sentences expand on the opening sentence. The last sentence sometimes draws a conclusion.

Opening sentences will be covered now. They must be made as concise and explicit as possible. Here are some examples of opening sentences that are too loose or contain unnecessary words, along with examples of their revisions:

Original Statement:

Dolphins seem to exhibit real intelligence.

Revision:

Dolphins are among the most intelligent of all mammals.

Original Statement:

There are many kinds of environmental pollution; they are all having a devastating impact on the world, some even more than others.

Revision:

Toxic waste and acid rain are having a devastating impact on the environment.

All of the revisions are more precisely stated than the original statements and will give the reader clues on what to expect from the supporting statements.

Another editing tip that can help you to create effective sentences and paragraphs is knowing where to put the emphasis in a sentence. Like everything else, a sentence has a beginning, middle, and end. Each position carries a different significance. In general, the least important position is in the middle, the second most important position is the beginning, and the most important position is the end. While this is not a rule, good writers usually emphasize their most important points by putting them at the end of sentences. In each of the following sentences the main point is not in a good position. An example of an appropriate revision follows each original sentence.

Original Sentence:

He tripped and fell as he approached the podium to make his speech.

Revision:

As he approached the podium to make his speech, he tripped and fell.

Original Sentence:

The Bensons lost their dining room chairs and table, some porcelain figurines, their dog, and some magazines when their home burned.

Revision:

When their home burned, the Bensons lost some magazines, some porcelain figurines, their dining room table and chairs, and their dog.

The original sentences are called loose sentences. The writer's ideas tumble along without regard for their position in the sentence and without regard for responsibility to the reader. In the revisions, the writer holds back the main point until just before the period. These revisions are called periodic sentences. Periodic sentences have two major purposes:

1. They use position to emphasize the most important point.
2. They convey a sense of order, a feeling that the writer is in control.

While periodic sentences are an excellent way to help the reader see the most important point of the sentence, they can be overused. If every sentence is periodic, the emphasis of the whole paragraph is diluted, and the writing seems stilted and contrived. The choice of when to use a periodic sentence depends upon the context and the writer's purpose. Good writers use them in moderation.

Here are two new proofreaders' marks for you to learn.

Proofreaders' Marks

⊐ Use this symbol to move text to the right.

⊏ Use this symbol to move text to the left.

Name _____ Date _____ Period _____

YOU, THE EDITOR!

Complete the following exercises to give you practice in writing more effective sentences and paragraphs. When you finish, write the date in the "Date Completed" column of your Work Assignment Log.

PART 1   CREATING STRONGER PARAGRAPHS

Instructions: Here are several paragraphs a customer has brought in. The topic sentence of each paragraph is weakly stated or in the wrong position for emphasis. Please edit the paragraphs so the reader will know what to expect after reading the opening sentence. Be sure to correct grammatical, spelling, punctuation, and other errors.

WHAT TO DO IN CaSE OF SNAKEBITE

If you are not sure whether a snakebite is poisonous, it is best to treat it as if it were poisonous. Although most snakes can bite, in the United States only copperheads, coral snakes, rattlesnakes, and water moccassins are poisonous. These snakes are more dangerous in the spring than at any other time of year. A poisonous snakebite is easy to recognize. The victim feels a throbbing pain raidiating from the bite. Within minutes, the wound will swelle and turn bright red. The pain and swelling wil gradually and steadily spread. Victims sometimes experience nausea and/or hot flashes.

Resist the temptation to walk or move quickly. Stay as quiet as possible. Do not take anything that could be

Continued

considered a stimulant such as coffee, tea, soft drinks containing caffeine, or aspirin. Avoid taking anything orally except a small amount of water. If you have been bitten, do nothing that could make the poison spread faster. Stay calm and don't panic.

To minimize the damage to the victim, follow these suggestioons. Keep the wound lower than the rest of the victim's body. Remain calm and move as little as possible. Arrange to get the victim to the hospital immediatrly. If it will take more than an hour to get the victim to the hospital, plce an icepack on the bite to slow down the spread of the poison. Remember, if you or anyone around you is bitten, the most important thing to do is to stay calm.

PART 2   APPLYING YOUR EDITING SKILLS

Instructions: Here is a document brought in by a customer. The subject of the document involves career opportunities in DTP. Please edit this document using everything you have learned about editing to date. After you have made editing changes on a copy of the document, copy the template disk file CAREERS and make the same changes to the file copy. Then print a revised copy of the document.

CAREER OPPORTUNITIES IN DESK TOP PUBLISHING

Every business in the United States is in the publishing business to one degree or another. Businesses publish

Continued

company newsletters to inform employees of things they should know. They create brochures about products and services. They publish company magazines, stockholders reports, special proposals for customers containing graphics, charts, and two- and three-column text. Companies that are currently using desk top publishing computer software include architectural firms, commercial art firms printing companies, publishing companies newspapers, and manufacturing companies. Elementary and secondary schools, adult schools, community colleges, and universities also use desk top publishing techniques to produce materials for the public.

It is a distinct advantage for an entry-level employee to be able to say, "I can use desk top publishing software as well as word processing, electronic spread sheet, and database management software. Job tiles for which such knowledge would be especialy advantageous include word processor, clerk-typist, and secretary. Employees in these positions find many occasions in which desk top publishing skills help them to produce communications that are effective in accomp[lishing the goals of the organization.

Current job market projections indicate that approximately 30 percent of the jobs available between now

Continued

and the turn of the century will be in the clerical and marketing fields. Almost everyone in these two categories will be interacting with a comuter in some way or another. Most clerical employees will have computers on their desks. If an employee has developed some desk top publishing skills along with the more traditional clerical skills expected, he or she will be more employable.

Find out more about desk top publishing. Contact your local high school or community college career center. Look for a program that teaches not only how to use the software, but, also, how to achieve an aesthetically pleasing layout, and how to edit to create good copy.

Don't be left behind! Get ready for the 21st century! Watch for new developments in computer software, such as desk top publishing, and then learn how to use them as effectively as possible.

Name _____ Date _____ Period _____

EXPLORING DESKTOP PUBLISHING

Omega needs some samples of good poster designs to show customers. Rudi wants you to make layout sketches and then desktop-publish two samples. In the following DTP activities, you will begin by experimenting with the graphic tools in your DTP software. Then apply what you learn to design and create the two posters.

When you finish each activity, write the date in the "Date Completed" column of your Work Assignment Log. By completing these activities, you will learn how to:

- Use the graphic tools that are available in your DTP software.
- Combine DTP graphics, text, and imported files for poster designs.
- Create poster designs for two different types of posters.

DTP ACTIVITY 7A   EXPERIMENTING WITH THE GRAPHIC TOOLS

Instructions: Load your DTP software and experiment with the graphic tools. Use each of the tools and the menu options, if possible. Try to perform these operations:

1. Draw straight vertical lines, horizontal lines, and lines at angles.
2. Draw freeform, curved lines.
3. Erase the lines.
4. Draw a box.
5. Change the line thickness of the box, or draw another box with a thicker line.
6. Make a shadow box for a name tag. Use the text tool to put your name in the shadow box.
7. Copy the shadow box. Put a friend's name in the new box.
8. Draw a circle. Use the freehand line tool to draw a face in the circle.
9. Select the circle and move it to another place on the page.
10. Use other special features of your DTP graphics. Write notes about the special features of your software in the space provided:

_____
_____
_____
_____
_____
_____
_____
_____

DTP ACTIVITY 7B   PREPARING THE CYCLE RACE POSTER

Instructions: The first sample poster you will create announces the Sunflower Time Trials, a race for amateur cycle enthusiasts. Rudi has prepared a graphic file, RACER, for it. Use the graphic tools in the desktop publishing software to enhance the poster design. Follow these steps:

1. Study the printout of the graphic file, RACER, and the text copy shown in step 2. If you are not using a template disk or if your software cannot import this file, obtain the copy of the RACER printout from Appendix B. Make at least three thumbnail sketches of the poster layout. Remember to use lines, boxes, and other shapes to help organize the information on the poster. Select type that will attract attention and that can be read from a distance.
2. Select one of your thumbnail sketches. Using it as a guide, prepare the poster. Key the following text directly into the DTP file:

```
Sunflower Time Trials
First rider off at 6:00 p.m., May 17, from Blue Fish Park
Draw lots for starting times
Five miles out and back
Flat to rolling hills, good pavement
Sponsored by the Santa Rosa Spinners
```

3. Print a proof copy of the poster. Put it on the wall or have someone hold it so you can examine it from a distance. Look for ways to improve the layout. You can cut up your proof copy to try out new ideas, then make the changes, and print a final copy.

DTP ACTIVITY 7C   PREPARING A POSTER ANNOUNCING DTP CLASSES

Instructions: The second sample poster you will create announces three desktop publishing classes that Omega will be offering in the evening. This is a different kind of poster—it consists only of text. Consider the different audience and type of information when you plan the poster. Follow these steps:

1. Review the text for the poster. If you are using a template disk, the text is in the file named CLASSES. Read the copy so that you will know the message that the poster is to communicate. Make at least three thumbnail sketches of layouts for the poster. Plan to use display type and the DTP graphic tools to organize the poster and to make it inviting to read.

2. Select one of your thumbnail sketches. Using it as a guide, prepare the poster. Import the CLASSES file. If you are not using a template disk, key the information. Use the skills you have learned for formatting type and text and for displaying the material in blocks.
3. Print a proof copy of the poster. Examine it from a distance. Look for ways to improve the layout. Make the changes and print a final copy.

An Invitation from Omega Desktop, Inc.

DESKTOP PUBLISHING CLASSES

Do you wonder what desktop publishing can do for you? Attend a series of three free classes designed to help you learn about desktop publishing. You will be introduced to desktop publishing software and equipment available to you at Omega Desktop, Inc. Each session is three hours long.

SESSION 1. May 12, 6:00-9:00 p.m. What is Desktop Publishing? Our staff will explain and demonstrate what desktop publishing software can do for you. Bring examples of publications you are interested in producing.

SESSION 2. May 26, 6:00-9:00 p.m. Preparing Documents for Desktop Publishing. In this session, you will learn how to prepare text and illustrations for documents you want to

Continued

desktop-publish. Our staff will explain rules and shortcuts for desktop publishing that will help transfer your files quickly into desktop-published documents.

SESSION 3. June 9, 6:00-9:00 p.m. Do-It-Yourself Desktop Publishing. Omega staff will be your tutors in basic desktop publishing skills. We will show you how to produce your own DTP documents on our equipment. Enrollment in this hands-on session is limited, so be sure to register early!

Complete a registration form for sessions you wish to attend. Ask our staff for the form and for additional information.

Name _____ Date _____ Period _____

VOCABULARY REVIEW

vo-cab-u-lary

The following terms are used in Chapter 7 and are defined in the Glossary. Match the definitions to the terms by placing the letter of the correct definition in the space provided. Review Chapter 7 or the Glossary for any terms you do not remember. Not all definitions will be used.

Terms

____ 1. paint program
____ 2. reverse
____ 3. shadow box
____ 4. fill pattern
____ 5. pixel
____ 6. draw program
____ 7. screen capture software
____ 8. file conversion software
____ 9. gray-mapped
____ 10. freehand

Definitions

A. use to draw attention to text
B. a single point or dot on the screen
C. changes file formats
D. white letters on a black background
E. to place behind an object
F. reproduces tones in a photograph
G. to draw without mechanical aids
H. creates object-oriented graphics
I. dots, lines, or colors used within a shape
J. creates bit-mapped graphics
K. takes a picture of the screen

TREASURE HUNT

Start a collection of brochures. You can pick up brochures almost anywhere—you might start with the counseling office or career center at your school. Look for brochures in these formats:

- Single and multiple pages.
- Folded in different ways.
- With and without illustrations.
- In different sizes and shapes.

Select at least two brochures that you like and that you think could be produced at Omega Desktop, Inc. Put these in your publishing handbook, along with thumbnail sketches of their layouts. In the next activity, you can refer to these for ideas as you experiment with the career opportunities brochure.

WORK ASSIGNMENT LOG

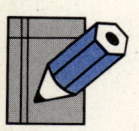

Fill in the "Date Assigned" and "Date Due" columns for each assignment that your teacher makes. When you complete an assignment, enter the date in the "Date Completed" column.

Chapter 7 Work Assignments	Date Assigned	Date Due	Date Completed
Software Check			
You, the Editor! Part 1			
You, the Editor! Part 2			
DTP Activity 7A			
DTP Activity 7B			
DTP Activity 7C			
Vocabulary Review			
Treasure Hunt			

Turn in Chapter 7 assignments after you have completed all of them, or follow your teacher's instructions. When these assignments are returned to you, put them in your publishing handbook.

CHAPTER 8
EXPERIMENTING WITH PAGE LAYOUT

CHAPTER OBJECTIVES

When you have completed this chapter, you will be able to:

- Use large initial caps and drop caps.
- Change text alignment.
- Create headers and footers.
- Use pull quotes and sidebars to set off text.
- Use a runaround to set off a picture.
- Adjust the layout and text for copyfitting.
- Edit to delete needless prefaces and modifiers.

INTRODUCTION

Andy Koyama is preparing for the classes Omega will be offering to customers. He has collected a stack of items that Omega has desktop-published. Leslie and Rudi are helping him pin them on the display board. Leslie points one out to you and Stan. "Here is your 'King of Rock' spread," he says. "Look at all these different layouts! There is certainly a lot of variety here."

You see several layout ideas you would like to try. One is a brochure that tells about a client's services. The first letter in each section is set in large type. Rudi explains that this is called a **large initial cap**. Sometimes the initial capital is set low so that the top of the letter is even with the top of the text. This is called a **drop cap**, because the large letter is lowered or dropped from the normal baseline. The use of the large first letter originated when manuscripts were lettered by hand, before type was invented.

Rudi has a page from a book that she designed. She used a one-column layout for the text with side heads. The **side heads** are in a narrow column on the left side of the text column. Each section side head begins at the same line as the first line of its section. Rudi likes this layout because it leaves white space on the page and the text in the single column is easy to read.

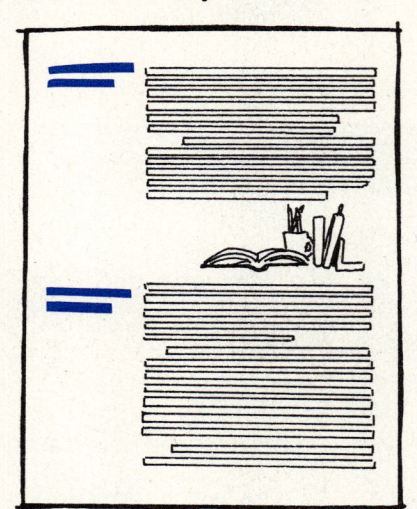

T his is an example of a large initial cap.

T his is an example of a drop cap. The initial letter is set below the first line.

R everse initial caps are sometimes used for the first character.

The book page also has headers and footers. A **header** is information that appears at the top of each page. There are headers in this book. They identify the chapter by its number and title. They help you locate the chapter. A **footer** is information that appears at the bottom of each page. The footer often contains the page number. The position of headers and footers must be planned as part of the page layout.

One of the newsletters in the display has fully justified text. When text is **justified**, the lines of type are spread so the margins on both sides of the column are even. You can justify text easily with the desktop publishing software. The same newsletter has **centered** heads. This

> **Pull quotes attract attention and tell the reader the main points in the article.**

means that the headings appear in the middle of the column or the page. The DTP software automatically places the heads in the middle of the column. Rudi has a title page that she designed for a book. The title is **flush right** or **right justified**—which means that the lines in the title all end at the right margin but are uneven on the left. Rudi says that these are examples of different **type alignments**, that is, the various ways that type can be placed or aligned. Each kind has an appropriate use.

In one of the newsletter articles, there is a short paragraph in the text that is set in large, bold type. The paragraph has a rule above it and below it. Rudi explains that this is called a pull quote. A **pull quote** is an important quotation from the text that has been selected and repeated in large type. Pull quotes attract attention and tell the reader the main points in the article.

Rudi points to the list of hit albums in your "King of Rock" spread. "Look," she says. "Here you have used an important layout device called a sidebar. Now that you know how to use the graphic tools, you could put a box around the sidebar. **Sidebars** contain additional information that helps to explain the main article. Often they are boxed or printed on a shaded background to set them off."

Stan is looking at a page of information about the local bus service. There is an illustration of a bus in the center of the page. The type is set to fit around the bus drawing. Rudi says that this is called a **runaround**. Some desktop publishing software makes it easy to fit lines of type to match the shape of an illustration.

> **MORE ABOUT SIDEBARS**
>
> This is an example of a sidebar. Unlike a pull quote, a sidebar does not repeat information from the main article. Instead, sidebars are used to give more details about the topic of the article or to explain a related subject. Sidebars are often used with magazine articles where they appear next to or below the main article.
>
> To set off the sidebar text from the main article, the text might be printed on a colored or shaded background. Sometimes a box is drawn around the sidebar. A different typeface and size can also be used.

Rudi asks, "Would you and Stan like to try publishing a brochure that uses some of these layout devices? Leslie and I have discussed some layout ideas. We like to work together so that each of us knows what the other person intends to do with the text and layout design. Remember, designing and writing both involve making decisions. Often Leslie and I can make better decisions if we talk over our ideas."

Leslie says, "We will turn the brochure job over to you. You may need to add to the text or delete some copy to make it fit the layout.

Maybe you can use some of it as a pull quote or sidebar. Plan the layout and copy fitting together."

Fill in the Work Assignment Log. Write the dates assigned and due dates for Chapter 8 work assignments. You will find the Work Assignment Log at the end of the chapter.

Name _____ Date _____ Period _____

SOFTWARE CHECK

Can you perform the following operations with your DTP software? If so, what menu or method do you use? Check your software manual or the information sheet that your teacher gives to you.

How do you format large initial caps? _____
_____
_____

How do you add drop caps? _____
_____
_____

How do you use headers and footers? _____
_____
_____

What are the commands to justify text? _____
_____
_____

What are the commands to right-justify text? _____
_____
_____

What are the commands to center text? _____
_____
_____

What are the commands to change column widths (as for a sidebar or side heads)?
_____
_____

What are the commands to run text around an illustration outline?
_____
_____

FACT SHEET: SPECIAL EFFECTS IN DESKTOP PUBLISHING

- Not all printers are capable of printing text with special effects such as reverses, rotated type, or very large display type. If this is the case with your printer, you may be able to create a bit-mapped graphic file that gives the same effect and that your printer is capable of producing. If your DTP software has paint tools, you can use them. If not, it is possible to use a separate paint program.

- In copy that is printed in a single color, shaded lines and boxes can give the effect of having a second color. For example, a light tint behind a sidebar helps to set it off from the rest of the text. Use very light shading behind text, so that the letters will be readable. Also consider using a larger type size and making the type bold.

- More and more publications are being printed in color. When color is used, most printing presses require a separate original, called a **color separation**, for each color. The original for each color prints only what will be printed in that specific color. This original is black on white, with the black showing where the color will be. New versions of desktop publishing software have features that help to make complex color separations. Simple color separations can be made easily with any DTP software package. Make a copy of the DTP file for each color. From each file copy, remove all but the parts that are to be printed in that color. Then print a copy of the file for each color.

- Inventing special effects to attract the reader is often a matter of experimenting with the tools your DTP software has available. These tools include cropping, sizing, and copying as well as adding type, lines, boxes, patterns, and other graphic elements.

AT THE EDITOR'S DESK

Leslie has some more editing suggestions for you. They concern modifiers. Modifiers are words, phrases, or clauses that alter the meaning of other sentence elements by limiting, describing, or emphasizing them. To modify means to qualify, to make more particular, or to specify more precisely. Using carefully chosen modifiers is another way to be concrete and specific with your writing. Problems with modifiers include:

Dangling Modifiers—When a sentence is written in such a way that the modifier cannot logically modify anything.

Example:

Driving down the freeway, my eyes burned from the smog.
(Those eyes must have looked strange driving by themselves!)

Correction:

As I drove down the freeway, the smog made my eyes burn.

Misplaced Modifiers—When the modifier is in the wrong place and seems to modify something else.

Example:

I asked her the next time to invite more interesting people.

Correction:

I asked her to invite more interesting people the next time.

Weak Modifiers—When the modifier is vague, redundant, or dull.

Example:

She has a nice car.

Correction:

She has a green Mercedes.

Example:

Last night we saw an interesting movie.

Correction:

Last night we watched an award-winning movie entitled Ben-Hur.

Some writers use needless prefaces. These writers start many of their sentences with words or phrases that are meaningless or redundant. A good editor will delete or replace these words or phrases to make the sentence stronger. Unnecessary phrases include:

	Delete/Replace With
as you may recall	*delete*
as you know	*delete*
you will remember	*delete*
due to the fact that	because
in regard to	about
in the event that	if

You can probably think of other unnecessary phrases to add to this list. Here is a good rule to follow: If the phrase does not add to the meaning of the sentence, it should be deleted or replaced with a more concrete word or phrase.

Here are two more proofreaders' marks for you to learn.

Proofreaders' Marks

‖Use this symbol to indicate that type needs to be aligned or set flush.

⌐ Use this symbol to move text ⌐up.⌐

Name _____   Date _____   Period _____

YOU, THE EDITOR!

A customer has brought in drafts of a letter and a notice. He wants you to edit them and print final copies. Revise the drafts to communicate more effectively.

PART 1   REWRITE TO COMMUNICATE MORE EFFECTIVELY

Instructions: Mark your changes on the printed copy. If you are using a template disk, update the file named BLAIRLTR and print a copy. If you are not using a template disk, key a copy with the changes you have made and print a copy.

Use today's date

Mr. Robert Blair
First United Bank
43251 Prospect Blvd.
Santa Rosa, CA 95405

Dear Mr. Blair

As you may recall, I spoke to you last month about the possibility of obtaining your support for our summer soccer league for children ages 6-12. Due to the fact that we have a much higher turnout than expected, we need to raise an additional $3,000 in donations and we need ten additional team coaches--three for girls' teams and seven for boys' teams.

Having previously expressed an interest in coaching, we thought you might be willing to take one of these teams. Please let me know as soon as possible if you can work this worthwhile volunteer effort into your busy schedule. Also, quite a few companies in town have made donations to support the program or assumed sponsorship of a team. Sponsors provide uniforms and equipment for their teams. Would First United Bank care to do so? Please call me at (787) 876-4300 with your answer.

Sincerely yours

Jonathan Morris, Director
Neighborhood Sports Project

PART 2   ANOTHER REWRITE TO COMMUNICATE MORE EFFECTIVELY

Instructions: Mark your changes on a printed copy of the flyer. Consider adding to the content of the flyer by incorporating information listed in the letter to Mr. Blair. If you are using a template disk, update the file named SOCCER. As you update the file, also center and bold the lines that are shown. Print a copy. If you are not using a template disk, key a copy with the changes you have made. Be sure to center and bold the lines as shown. Print a copy. If you have time, use your DTP software to create an attractive copy of this flyer and print it.

```
                    SUMMER SOCCER LEAGUE
                            FOR
                   BOYS AND GIRLS, AGES 6-12


INFORMATION FOR PARENTS

Sign ups will take place in all city parks on Tuesdays and
Thursdays between 3:30 and 5:00 p.m.  Parents must accompany
their children to enroll.

Teams will be put together on June 15 and practice will start
on June 17.  League play will begin on July 15.

Parent volunteers are needed.  Uniforms will be provided free
by team sponsors.  Children must make the commitment to play
the season--June 17 through August 15.  There will be two
games per week.  Teams that win their league championships
will be expected to participate in the playoffs.  Parents who
plan to take out-of-town vacations during this time are asked
not to enroll their children in the program as their absence
will create a hardship for the rest of the children on the
team.
```

Name _____ Date _____ Period _____

EXPLORING DESKTOP PUBLISHING

Complete the following activities to learn more about special effects in layouts. When you complete each activity, write the date in the "Date Completed" column of your Work Assignment Log. By completing these activities, you will learn how to:

- Change the alignment of text.
- Use special effects.
- Plan a brochure layout that fits the copy, and edit copy to fit the layout.

DTP ACTIVITY 8A   EXPERIMENTING WITH TEXT ALIGNMENT AND SPECIAL EFFECTS

Instructions: You can use some of your earlier projects to experiment with special effects. Here is a list of things to try on the "King of Rock" article:

1. Box the album information to create a true sidebar.
2. Begin the article with a drop cap.
3. Change the text alignment so that it is justified.
4. Select a quotation from the article and set it as a pull quote.
5. Run text around the guitar illustration.
6. Create a footer that identifies the publication as AIRWAYS and the issue as November 1990.

Print your completed experiments.

DTP ACTIVITY 8B   PLANNING A CAREERS BROCHURE

Instructions: For this project, you will create a brochure describing career opportunities in desktop publishing. Use the CAREERS text file you edited for Chapter 7. The illustrations for the brochure are named DTP1 and DTP2 on your template disk. If you are not using a template disk, use the copies printed in Appendix B.

Remember, you can add to the text or edit it to fit the layout you plan. For example, you might add a sidebar that describes a particular job in desktop publishing or tells about the training in the class. You might add heads to identify the main sections. You also might copy, crop, or resize the illustrations.

Consider the capabilities of your DTP software when you plan the brochure layout. Create at least three sketches with the following specifications in mind.

1. *Page Size and Orientation.* Plan the brochure for 8½ by 11-inch paper printed on two sides (back-to-back). If your DTP software can

use a landscape orientation, plan the brochure in landscape format. If your software uses only portrait orientation, you have two options: use manual pasteup to create a horizontal layout, or plan the brochure in portrait orientation.
2. *Folds*. Plan the brochure to be divided into three **panels**. Panels are printed sections separated by space where the paper will be folded. When the sheet is folded twice to make three equal-sized panels on each side, it will fit easily into a business envelope for mailing.
3. *Margins and Columns*. When planning margins, consider the amount of text, type sizes, heads, illustrations, and other graphic devices you want to use. Plan column widths that are easy to read and that fit well in the three-fold format.
4. *Type Selection*. Refer to your type sample sheets when you select type and type sizes. Remember to consider leading, line length, and alignment when you specify type for the title, heads, and body text.
5. *Illustrations*. Decide upon the size and space the illustrations are to occupy. Consider repeating parts of the illustrations on each side of the brochure page, perhaps in different sizes.
6. *Special Effects*. Consider using some of the special effects that are described in this chapter.

When you have completed the sketches, select one and prepare the brochure according to this layout. Print a proof copy and adjust the layout. Then print the brochure in its final form.

Name Date Period

VOCABULARY REVIEW

The following terms are used in Chapter 8 and are defined in the Glossary. Match the definitions to the terms by placing the letter of the correct definition in the space provided. Review Chapter 8 or the Glossary for any terms you do not remember. Not all definitions will be used.

Terms

___ 1. drop cap
___ 2. side heads
___ 3. centered
___ 4. justified
___ 5. type alignment
___ 6. sidebar
___ 7. pull quote
___ 8. runaround
___ 9. footer
___ 10. color separation

Definitions

A. a selected portion of text set in large type

B. justified, centered, flush right, flush left

C. a block of text containing additional information

D. an original for each color

E. heads set to the left of the text, not above the text

F. a large initial letter set to align at the top with the first text line

G. the lines of type are even on the right and left

H. the lines of type are in the middle of the column

I. type line lengths are adjusted to fit the shape of a picture

J. the lines of type are flush to the right

K. a line that appears at the bottom of every page

TREASURE HUNT

Have you noticed how many different kinds of printed materials people use? Start collecting examples of all the printed items that Omega might produce or use in the shop. Look for these examples and any others that you can think of:

- Signs, announcements, and posters.
- Order forms, receipts, and invoices.
- Letterhead, envelopes, and business cards.
- Reports, catalogs, and instruction manuals.

Decide on a single-page item that you would like to desktop-publish to use as a sample for Omega customers. Collect variations of this item. For instance, if you want your project to be a new order form for the shop, find several different examples of order forms that you can study for ideas in setting up your new form.

WORK ASSIGNMENT LOG

Fill in the "Date Assigned" and "Date Due" columns for each assignment that your teacher makes. When you complete an assignment, enter the date in the "Date Completed" column.

Chapter 8 Work Assignments	Date Assigned	Date Due	Date Completed
Software Check			
You, the Editor! Part 1			
You, the Editor! Part 2			
DTP Activity 8A			
DTP Activity 8B			
Vocabulary Review			
Treasure Hunt			

Turn in Chapter 8 assignments after you have completed all of them, or follow your teacher's instructions. When these assignments are returned to you, put them in your publishing handbook.

CHAPTER 9
DEVELOPING PRODUCTS FOR OMEGA DESKTOP, INC.

CHAPTER OBJECTIVES

When you have completed this chapter, you will be able to:

✔ Ask the right questions when planning a publication.

✔ Use special features of your desktop publishing software to prepare makeovers, comprehensives, and mechanicals.

✔ Create a variety of desktop-published products on your own.

✔ Edit to vary sentence structure and length.

✔ Apply basic word division rules.

✔ Combine related thoughts and use short sentences for emphasis.

INTRODUCTION

Aiko and Andy are pleased about the success of the Omega desktop publishing classes. "A lot of our customers learned more about desktop publishing," Aiko says. "Now they have a better idea about all the different products we can help them make. Our business has improved already. We will be busier than ever."

Leslie and Rudi agree. They each have a pile of job orders on their desks. "We're glad you and Stan have experience with editing and desktop publishing," Leslie tells you. "Both of you are ready to take on some of these projects on your own. Rudi and I will help you get started."

Rudi explains that there are some important practical questions to ask when you are starting work on any publication:

- What is the purpose of the publication?
- What are the contents of the publication?
- Who is the audience? Who will read or use the publication?
- How much time will they want to spend reading or using it?
- How much time do you have to produce the publication?
- What resources do you have for producing it?
- How much does the customer want to spend?

Leslie agrees that these questions can apply to any project. As an example, Rudi tells you how she has approached her current job. Dr. Dallas, a new Omega customer, has ordered business cards. The purpose of the cards is to give other people facts about Dr. Dallas that they can take with them. The contents include her name, address, phone number, and the name of her dental clinic. The audience consists of people she meets. While they will spend only a few seconds reading the business card, they may want to put it away with other cards for future reference. Dr. Dallas needs the cards in two weeks so that she will have them while attending a convention in St. Louis. Rudi can use any of Omega's software and hardware to compose the cards, but Omega will not print them in house. Rudi must allow time to send them to the printer. Because Dr. Dallas wants these to be attractive cards, she is willing to pay for special paper and two-color printing.

Leslie says, "I can see that you would use a standard business card size so that the card can be kept with others. To make it stand out, however, what if it were printed on a colored paper stock?"

Rudi thinks that is a good idea. She will choose a color that suits Dr. Dallas's professional image. She has selected a typeface that is easy to read in small sizes.

Rudi has also designed matching letterhead and envelopes for Dr. Dallas. She shows you the **comps**, or finished layout samples she will show Dr. Dallas for her approval. *Comp* is short for **comprehensive**. Unlike thumbnail sketches, the comprehensives are carefully made to closely resemble the final products. Rudi uses the DTP software and adds the second color by hand. When customers see their ideas in this form, they can visualize how the printed copy will look. At this stage customers can still make changes that are easy to incorporate.

After Dr. Dallas approves the comp, Rudi will use DTP software to make the **camera-ready copy**—that is, the original work used as a master for reproducing copies. A camera-ready copy is also called a **mechanical**. The printer will photograph the mechanicals to produce a matched set of cards and stationery.

Rudi shows you the project she is working on now. It is a revision, or **makeover**, of a client's resume. The old resume was typed on a typewriter. With Leslie's help, the client has made changes to improve the resume. Now Rudi will desktop-publish the resume. She will choose typefaces, sizes, and styles to help the reader recognize the important information in the resume. She has also planned to add graphic elements that will make the layout more attractive.

Leslie reminds you that there is a lot of other work to be edited and desktop-published. There are several newspaper ads to be produced. The Lamppost Restaurant wants handouts prepared that can be distributed at the motels that are near the restaurant. The principal at the new elementary school has ordered name tags for the teachers to wear at the open house. The publicity chairperson of the coming county fair has ordered small posters, signs, and promotional flyers. The MG Classics Car Club has brought in an order, and the local computer users' group needs help with publishing its newsletter. Andy wants to promote Omega's business by giving customers a free list of all the state postal abbreviations, and Omega needs a revised price list and an order form.

You are pleased that Rudi and Leslie think you are able to do these jobs on your own. When Rudi says that some of the projects may require using features of the desktop publishing software you have not used yet, you feel confident that you can find the instructions in the software manuals and information sheets.

Fill in the Work Assignment Log. Write the dates assigned and due dates for Chapter 9 work assignments. You will find the Work Assignment Log at the end of the chapter.

Name _____   Date _____   Period _____

SOFTWARE CHECK

✓

Every DTP software package has special features that make it unique. Read this chapter's Fact Sheet for descriptions of some special features your software may have. Find out if you can perform the operations using your software. If so, what menu or procedure do you use? What other special features have you used in your software or read about in the manual?

How do you control letterspacing? _____
_____
_____

How do you kern letter pairs? _____
_____
_____

Does your software have a snap-to grid? _____
How do you use it? _____
_____
_____

How do you make snapshots of the screen? _____
_____
_____

How do you **skew** or distort images? _____
_____
_____

How do you set up style sheets? _____
_____
_____

Other special features of your software: _____
_____
_____
_____
_____
_____
_____
_____
_____

FACT SHEET:
DESKTOP PUBLISHING SOFTWARE FEATURES

- In many DTP packages, you can control the spacing between letters. **Letterspacing** can be critical when text is justified. To make the left and right margins even, there may be large gaps between words. The word spacing can be improved by adding small amounts of space between the letters.

- DTP software may automatically **kern** certain pairs of letters. This means that two letters, such as T and o, are automatically brought closer together, so that the left side of the o is under the top of the T. Without kerning, the two letters would appear to have extra space between them because of their shapes. Other examples of kerned pairs are Yo, We, Tr, VA, and YO. Look for other examples of kerned pairs. You may be able to kern letters manually as well. Kerning is most obvious in larger type sizes.

You Try

You Try

- A grid pattern can be a useful guide for arranging type and graphics on a page. The grid can be a visible or an invisible pattern of horizontal and vertical lines. In some software a **snap-to grid** can be set to act like a magnet. The snap-to grid aligns type and graphics on the screen. When you use the mouse, you can actually feel a snap-to grid pull the text or graphic elements into alignment at the grid lines.

- Many desktop publishing programs will automatically hyphenate words that are too long to fit at the end of a line. The programs use a hyphenation dictionary that is part of the software. When hyphens are used to fit part of a word at the end of a line, the line can be justified without inserting large blank spaces between the words. If the software does not hyphenate words, they must be hyphenated manually. As a general rule, there should be no more than two lines in a row that end in hyphenated words. With some DTP software, you can control the number of successive lines that are hyphenated.

AT THE EDITOR'S DESK

Leslie mentions that he has not yet discussed **hyphenation**, or using the hyphen to divide words at the end of a line. Some desktop publishing and word processing programs will divide words at the end of a line automatically. However, some will not. For this reason, it is important to remember a few basic rules about word division.

1. Always divide words between syllables.
2. When in doubt, look up the word in a dictionary or in a word-division manual.
3. Never divide a one-syllable word.
4. Never divide a word immediately after a one-letter syllable. For example, do not divide *again* as *a-gain*.

Leslie tells you that now you are getting to the interesting part of editing—the part that requires analyzing and thinking. When you edit, first read the entire text. Ask yourself, "Does this make sense? Can I make changes that will make it easier for the audience to understand the message? Is the text interesting? Can I change the sentences or reorganize paragraphs to make the document more interesting?"

Leslie points out that some writers use long, complicated sentences while others use short sentences. Either style becomes dull when there is no variety in sentence structure and length.

When editing, analyze the entire page. Are there both long and short sentences? Are some of the sentences complex and some simple? If not, rewrite some of the sentences so you have sentences of different lengths.

Many good writers and editors use short sentences for emphasis or to make a point. When editing, determine the point the writer is trying to make and consider whether it would be more effective to use a short sentence to call attention to or **emphasize** that point.

Example:

Computers are changing our lives in many ways: the way we perform our jobs, the way we make financial transactions, the way we make purchases, and the way we communicate.

Revision:

Computers are changing our lives. These changes include the way we communicate, make financial transactions, make purchases, and perform our jobs.

If you are editing a document made up almost entirely of short sentences, you can add variety and interest by combining several related thoughts into one medium or long sentence.

Example:

I was a lifeguard last summer. I discovered that people are often rude. They are rude even when they owe you their life.

Revision:

While working as a lifeguard last summer, I discovered that people are often rude—even when they owe you their life.

Though this is a long sentence, it still flows better than it did as three sentences.

Imagine how the words will sound when spoken. Do the sentences create vivid word pictures in your mind? Can you make the sentences sound better by modifying them in some way? These are the things to consider when you edit.

Here are two more proofreaders' marks for you to learn.

Proofreaders' Marks

⊔   Use this symbol to indicate a word that should be moved down.

=   Use this symbol to indicate where a hyphen should be added. (Example: spur of the moment party)

Name _____ Date _____ Period _____

YOU, THE EDITOR!

Leslie remarks that you are getting more skilled at editing each day you work. Here are two more editing assignments for you. The second one is more challenging than the first.

PART 1   EDITING A MANUSCRIPT

Instructions: Leslie tells you that before you came to work for Omega, he edited an art textbook. It was printed as camera-ready copy and sent to Dr. Olvera at the community college. Dr. Olvera has returned a page of text that contains some incorrect word divisions at the end of several lines. Please mark this copy so it can be keyed correctly. Make sure that any divided words follow the rules discussed in this chapter.

```
                              Masks

Masks are an especially beautiful art form with an interes-
ting history.  Almost all primitive cultures, from prehis-
toric times until the present, used masks.  American Indian
cultures have used masks in ceremonies to ward off evil spir-
its, to cure sickness, to bring rain, to make crops grow, and
to create a climate of harmony and good will.

Masks are made from a variety of materials.  Some, like many
African masks, are made of wood.  Others, like many American
Indian masks, are sewn of leather, feathers, and fur.  Masks
from some ancient Central and South American and Egyptian cult-
ures are made of gold and platinum alloys and are encrusted
with precious jewels.

Museums of natural history throughout the United States invar-
iably have a collection of masks on display.  Most of them
have been selected for display because of the precious metals
from which they are made or for the fine workmanship and
artistry that went into their creation.

Since art collectors have long been interested in masks, man-
y of today's young artists see the creating of masks as an
exciting medium of expression.  The most highly prized of the-
se current masks are those that are evocative of ancient cul-
tures.  While many of today's masks express space-age topics,
a close examination will probably show their connection to
their primitive roots.
```

163

PART 2   EDITING TO IMPROVE SENTENCE FLOW

Instructions: One of Omega's customers has brought in the following paragraph to be edited. It is from a new publication on computer use. There are several short sentences that could be combined. Also, make sure that ideas are expressed clearly and that relationships between ideas are expressed accurately. Reword as much as necessary to create clear, concise copy containing sentences of different lengths. Be sure to correct all misspelled words.

In many situations home computers are essential. In large cities traffic will become heavier. It is certain to be more frustrating to move around. Americans in the near future may prefer to wrok from home. That way, they can avoid the traffic. It will cut expenses of getting to work also. If more people are able to work from home, it wall also cut donw on smog. Home computers have ssemed like a luxury to most poeple; in the future, they will be a necessity. For a small percentage of the workforce, there may be not option. They may be forced to get a home computer in order to earn a living.

Name _____ Date _____ Period _____

EXPLORING DESKTOP PUBLISHING

Select several desktop publishing projects you want to attempt on your own or as a team activity. Select your projects from these sources:

1. From the Omega job orders on the following pages. The files listed on the job orders are on the template disk. Obtain printouts of graphic files from Appendix B if you are not using a template disk or if your software cannot import the graphic files.
2. From the desktop publishing examples you have collected. Do a makeover of one example.
3. Invent a project of your own or do a project for someone you know.

For each project, first answer the planning questions. Then draw thumbnails and make a comprehensive layout of the one you decide to produce. Have the comp approved and then prepare the finished camera-ready copy. By following these steps, you will learn to:

■ Consider the right questions and make appropriate decisions concerning the design and production of a publication.

■ Prepare thumbnails and a sample comprehensive layout for the customer's approval.

■ Complete the project using desktop publishing methods.

Omega DTP Job Order

Client: *Andy*
Today's date: _____
Date due: _____
Description: *List of State Abbreviations Format for printing two-up on 8½×11-inch paper. (Andy suggests a vertical list instead of three columns - Rudi)*

Files: *STATES*

Add this text at the bottom of the STATES list:

Printed for you by Omega Desktop, Inc.

```
STATE ABBREVIATIONS

AL    Alabama          LA    Louisiana         OH    Ohio
AK    Alaska           ME    Maine             OK    Oklahoma
AZ    Arizona          MD    Maryland          OR    Oregon
AR    Arkansas         MA    Massachusetts     PA    Pennsylvania
CA    California       MI    Michigan          RI    Rhode Island
CO    Colorado         MN    Minnesota         SC    South Carolina
CT    Connecticut      MS    Mississippi       SD    South Dakota
DE    Delaware         MO    Missouri          TN    Tennessee
FL    Florida          MT    Montana           TX    Texas
GA    Georgia          NE    Nebraska          UT    Utah
HI    Hawaii           NV    Nevada            VT    Vermont
ID    Idaho            NH    New Hampshire     VA    Virginia
IL    Illinois         NJ    New Jersey        WA    Washington
IN    Indiana          NM    New Mexico        WV    West Virginia
IA    Iowa             NY    New York          WI    Wisconsin
KS    Kansas           NC    North Carolina    WY    Wyoming
KY    Kentucky         ND    North Dakota
```

Omega DTP Job Order

Client: Lamppost Restaurant
Today's date: _____
Date due: _____
Description: Flyer for motel distribution. Combine text and graphic files. Client says, "Layout is up to you!"

Files: LAMPTEXT (text)
LAMPPOST (graphic)

Welcome to Santa Rosa and The LAMPPOST RESTAURANT

879 Eldorado Blvd., Santa Rosa
(787) 436-0967

SPECIALIZING IN SEAFOOD AND SALADS
Open for lunch and dinner
11:00 a.m. - 10:00 p.m. Tuesday through Sunday

The Lamppost is a Santa Rosa landmark. Since 1949, we have served local residents and visitors from throughout the world. We pride ourselves on our reasonably priced selection of classic seafood and salad dishes, as well as our own unique dishes that are favorites with our customers. We invite you to stop by while you are in Santa Rosa. If you can't make it this trip, take this Lamppost recipe with you and plan to visit us the next time you are in town.

Lamppost Seafood Salad - A luncheon for four
1/2 pound white crab meat
3/4 pound shrimp
1 apple diced
3/4 cup cooked rice
2 hard-boiled eggs chopped
1/4 pound medium cheddar cheese cubed
1/4 cup Lamppost basil mayonnaise
1 heaping tablespoon Dijon mustard
Season to taste with salt, pepper, curry, and garlic salt.
Mix together and serve chilled in lettuce cups.

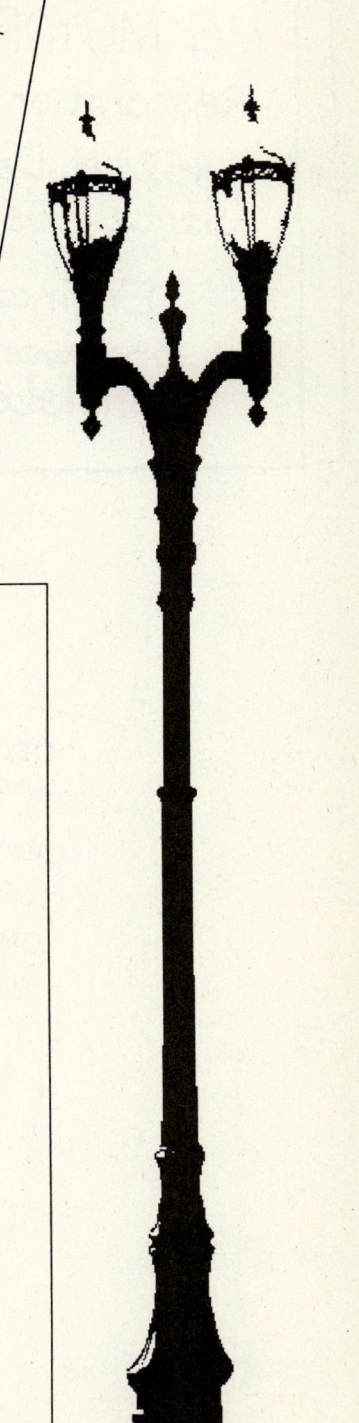

←— 4¼" —→

MG MOTOR CLASSICS
Restoration Specialists
4521 N. Delancy
Santa Rosa, CA

Engines
Bodywork
Upholstery

↕ 4"

Omega DTP Job Order

Client: **MG Motor Classics**
Today's date: _____
Date due: _____
Description: **Prepare camera-ready ad — 4¼" x 4" final size. See layout attached (OK to modify).**

Use MG illustration

Files: **MG (graphic)**

Omega DTP Job Order

Client: <u>Morgan Elementary School</u>
Today's date: _____
Date due: _____
Description: <u>Name tags to fit 3¾" × 2½" plastic holder. Print eight-up on 8½×11-inch paper. Use border on each tag to guide cutting. Need camera-ready copy. (See layout.)</u>

Files: <u>BELL (graphic) on each name tag</u>

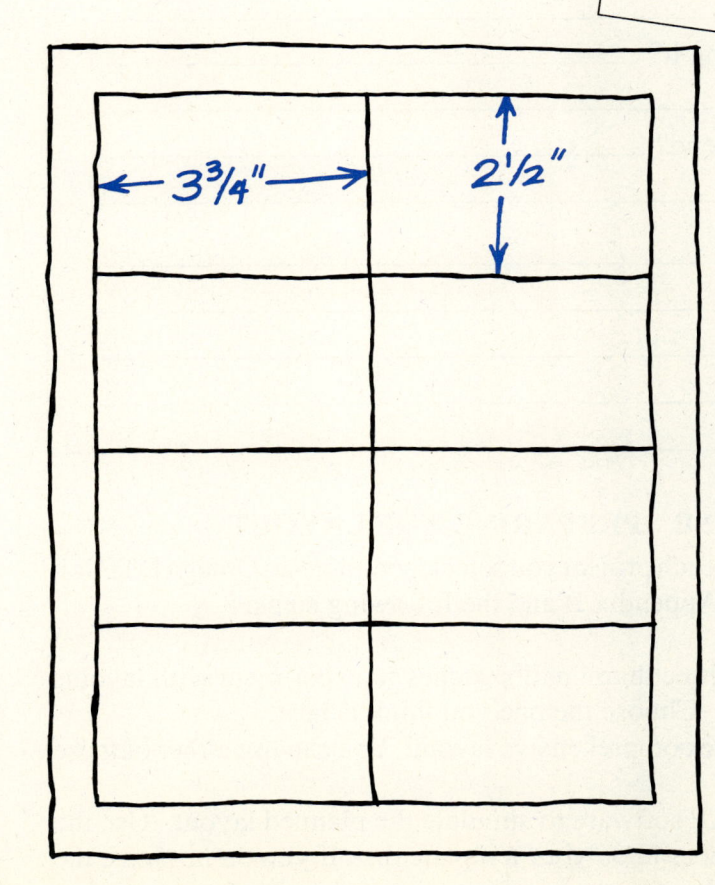

Text:
Welcome to
Morgan Elementary School
My name is

DTP ACTIVITY 9A   ANSWERING THE PLANNING QUESTIONS

Instructions: For each project you select, write the answers to the following questions. Note how you think your answers might affect the way you produce the project. If the project is for another person, discuss the answers with your "client."

Project Planning Worksheet

Project title: _____

1. What is the purpose of the publication? _____
   _____

2. What are the contents of the publication? _____
   _____

3. Who is the audience? Who will read or use the publication? ____
   _____

4. How much time will they want to spend reading or using it? ____
   _____

5. How much time do you have to produce the publication? _____
   _____

6. What resources do you have for producing it? _____
   _____

7. How much does the customer want to spend? _____
   _____

How will this affect the publication? _____
_____
_____
_____

DTP ACTIVITY 9B   PREPARING THE LAYOUT

Instructions: For each project you select, complete an Omega DTP Job Order Form from Appendix B and the following steps:

1. Draw at least three thumbnail sketches to experiment with layouts you might use. Choose the one you think is best.
2. Make a full-size comprehensive layout. You can use either of these methods:
   a. Use the DTP software to simulate the planned layout. Use the text file SIMULATE on your template disk if you do not have the final text file. Print a proof copy.

b. If it is more convenient for you to work away from the computer, simulate the layout by pasting up type blocks clipped from a magazine or by drawing lines to indicate the blocks of text.
3. Add color (if any) with colored pencils, paints, pastels, or ink. Sketch in any elements you plan to add, such as photographs, artwork, or large type that must be pasted up.
4. Have your client approve the comprehensive layout.

DTP ACTIVITY 9C   DESKTOP-PUBLISHING THE DOCUMENT

Instructions: When the comp is approved, prepare the camera-ready copy using the DTP software. For places where you intend to insert art or photos you do not have as computer files, use the DTP graphic tools to draw **placeholders**. Placeholders are empty boxes that show where a graphic or text block will go. After you print your publication, manually paste up any type or graphic elements that you could not import into the desktop publishing software. These might include large type, rotated type, or graphics that are not available as disk files.

Name _____ Date _____ Period _____

VOCABULARY REVIEW

vo·cab·u·lary

The following terms are used in Chapter 9 and are defined in the Glossary. Match the definitions to the terms by placing the letter of the correct definition in the space provided. Review Chapter 9 or the Glossary for any terms you do not remember. Not all definitions will be used.

Terms

____ 1. makeover
____ 2. comprehensive
____ 3. skew
____ 4. hyphenation
____ 5. snap-to grid
____ 6. letterspacing
____ 7. mechanical
____ 8. placeholder
____ 9. emphasize
____ 10. kern

Definitions

A. shows where a graphic will go
B. the final pasteup used for reproduction
C. the distance between letters in words
D. to make a point
E. a revised version of a publication
F. to adjust spacing between a letter pair
G. used to align elements on the page
H. to distort
I. first line in a column
J. dividing words at the end of lines
K. layout that closely resembles the final product

TREASURE HUNT

You are about to begin your final project for Omega—the *Omega Desktop, Inc., Publishing Handbook*. One of the most important steps will be to design a cover for the handbook. Start collecting ideas for the cover. Look at cover designs on reports and manuals in the library and at bookstores. Make thumbnails of covers that appeal to you and that you think could be produced with desktop publishing. If possible, photocopy two or three covers or bring the originals to show the class.

Another important part of your handbook will be the table of contents. Look for examples of ways such tables are set up in manuals and books. If possible, photocopy examples that seem especially well done and bring your copies (or the originals) to class.

WORK ASSIGNMENT LOG

Fill in the "Date Assigned" and "Date Due" columns for each assignment that your teacher makes. When you complete an assignment, enter the date in the "Date Completed" column.

Chapter 9 Work Assignments	Date Assigned	Date Due	Date Completed
Software Check			
You, the Editor! Part 1			
You, the Editor! Part 2			
DTP Activity 9A			
DTP Activity 9B			
DTP Activity 9C			
Vocabulary Review			
Treasure Hunt			

Turn in the Chapter 9 assignments after you have completed all of them, or follow your teacher's instructions. When these assignments are returned to you, put them in your publishing handbook.

CHAPTER 10
CREATING A PUBLISHING HANDBOOK

CHAPTER OBJECTIVES

When you have completed this chapter, you will be able to:

✔ Design and publish a cover for the handbook.

✔ Create and publish a title page.

✔ Organize and publish a table of contents.

✔ Edit text for good organization.

INTRODUCTION

Andy has asked you and Stan to come into his office. He tells you to sit down and then sits behind his desk. Andy explains that business has been going so well at Omega Desktop that he and Aiko have decided to hire four new part-time employees. Although this is a step forward, Andy is afraid that he will not be able to find people who are well trained in desktop publishing. He tells you and Stan, "There is so much to learn about this field. I wish there were more people out there who have your experience and training. I think you could help us out.

"You have done a lot of work to learn editing skills from Leslie. You have made different types of desktop publications and have learned about layout and design from Rudi. You have collected examples of type, layouts, and desktop publishing products. I would like you to organize your work into a publishing handbook we can show to new employees. If our new employees could look at your work, I am sure they would learn from it."

You and Stan are pleased that Andy thinks your work would help others to learn desktop publishing. You ask how you can help produce the handbook.

Andy gives you a list of the items he thinks should be in the handbook. They are all work assignments you have done at Omega.

"I would like you to design a cover for the handbook. You can use the Omega logo if you like, or you can design a logo or graphic of your own. Put the title of the handbook and the author's name on the cover. You are the author! The handbook should also have a **title page**. Put the handbook title and the author's name there. Often you can use the same type selections and arrangement for both the cover and the title page. For example, you might just make the type on the title page smaller than on the cover. Other information you might find on a title page of a publication includes the city and state where the book is published and the name of the publisher."

Then Andy describes the table of contents. He says that you need to review all of the items on the list he has given you and decide how to organize them in the handbook. He suggests several alternatives. One idea is to put the editing exercises together in one section, the desktop publishing activities in another section, and the materials you have collected in a third section. Another idea is to arrange the materials in the order in which you produced and gathered them.

When you have decided upon an arrangement to use, Andy advises you to organize the pages in that order and number them. Start numbering with the first page of your first section, using Arabic numerals (1, 2, 3, etc.). If you were desktop-publishing the handbook from the beginning, you could add the page number, or **folio**, with the desktop publishing software. Instead, you can type or write the number neatly on each page. You might decide to add the page number at the upper corner or center it at the bottom of the page.

Next make a list of the topics and their page numbers for a table of contents page. If possible, originate the list with a word processing program or directly with desktop publishing software. Use dot leaders between the section names and the page numbers. A **dot leader** is a row of periods used to fill the space between a line of text and a number in a chart or table of contents. The dot leader helps the reader find the number that is on the same line as the text.

Sometimes books have other **front matter**. This is the name given to the title page, table of contents, and other pages that appear before the first section or chapter. There might also be a **preface**, as there is in this book. The preface contains an introduction that tells the purpose of the book and describes its features. You can write a short preface for your handbook if you wish. When you have finished all of the front matter pages, you can number them using lowercase Roman numerals (i, ii, iii, etc.). Count the title page as page i but do not put a page number on it.

Books often have appendices. These are sections at the end of the book that contain reference information. Your DTP software manual may have appendices also. Usually appendices are identified by letter (A, B, C, etc.) rather than by numbers. Each appendix has a special purpose or subject. You may want to put your Treasure Hunt materials in appendices at the back of your publishing handbook. You can start the page numbering for each appendix with page 1. You can identify each page by both the appendix and by the page number. This will make it easy to add pages to the appendices if you want to expand your publishing handbook later. This will also help identify in which appendix a particular page should be inserted if it has been removed from the handbook for any reason.

"We need to decide how to bind the handbook," Andy says. He shows you some books with different styles of bindings. One has a plastic comb binding and another has a wire spiral binding. **Comb bindings** hold pages together with curled plastic strips, and **spiral bindings** use a spiral curl of wire to hold pages together. These bindings make it easy to open publications and to lay them flat. They can even be folded back with the open page exposed like a book cover. Another binding, **saddle stitching**, is popular for thinner books and booklets. The printed pages are folded somewhat like a newspaper. The pages are held together with staple-like wire in the fold. The wire, usually on a spool, is cut to the desired length. Omega has equipment to do comb binding and saddle stitching.

Another type is the paper-bound book with a **perfect binding**. With this type of binding, the cover is wrapped around the book's **spine**, and the inside edges of the pages are glued to the cover. The spine of a book is the part where the pages are held together. Many magazines have perfect bindings. This book has a perfect binding.

Andy thinks the best way to bind Omega's publishing handbook is to put the pages in a loose-leaf binder. Then you can add to them easily later. **Drill** or punch holes in the pages so they will fit in the binder. Omega has a special machine that can drill holes similar to those made by a three-hole punch.

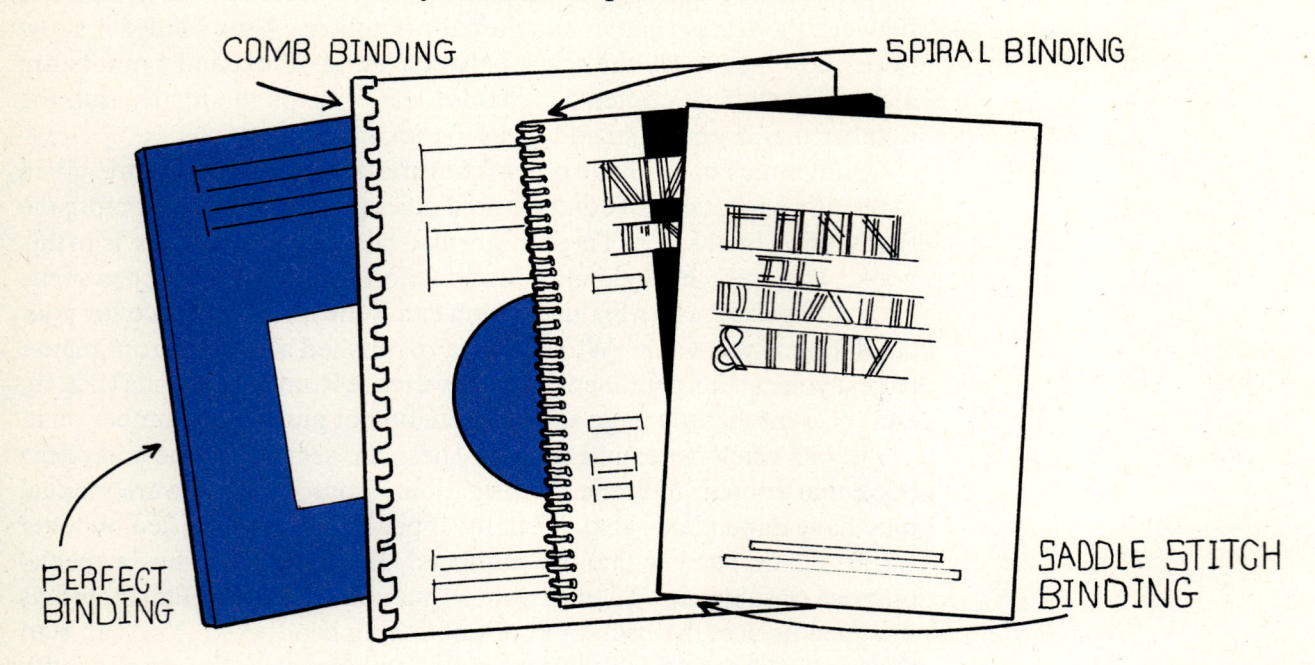

COMB BINDING
SPIRAL BINDING
PERFECT BINDING
SADDLE STITCH BINDING

Fill in the Work Assignment Log. Write the dates assigned and due dates for Chapter 10 work assignments. You will find the Work Assignment Log at the end of the chapter.

Name _____ Date _____ Period _____

SOFTWARE CHECK

By this time, you have a good working knowledge of your desktop publishing software. To know how it compares with other DTP software and to learn about options available with other packages, complete the chart below. Write the name of your software at the top of column 1. Select two other DTP software packages and write their names at the top of columns 2 and 3. In each column, check the tasks that can be done with that software. To find out about the other software, consult books and magazine articles about the software in your library, ask users of the software, or try out the software if copies are available for your use.

Comparison of Desktop Publishing Programs

DTP Tasks	_____ (Your Software)	_____ (Other Software Package)	_____ (Other Software Package)
Can you show pages at different sizes?			
Can you show a view of facing pages?			
Can you do landscape and portrait orientation?			
Can you use a snap-to grid?			
Can you rotate type?			
Can you reverse type?			
What are the maximum number of columns?			
Can you edit graphics?			
Can you import object-oriented graphics?			
Can you select fill patterns?			

Continued

DTP Tasks	(Your Software)	(Other Software Package)	(Other Software Package)
Can you select line weights?			
Can you repeat headers and footers?			
Can you make screen shots?			
Can you automatically hyphenate words?			
Can you do kerning and letterspacing?			
Other _____			
_____			
_____			
_____			

FACT SHEET: COMPLETING THE PUBLICATION PROCESS

- Developing a table of contents or index is always one of the last steps in preparing a book, catalog, or similar publication. The page numbers must be set before the table of contents or index can be made. Some sophisticated desktop publishing software will automatically produce the table of contents and index from codes that are entered in the text. The codes identify the headings and terms that should appear in the table of contents and/or the index. The DTP software combines the marked information with the page number where it appears to create the table of contents and index.

- When several copies of a multiple-page document are printed, the pages for each copy must be arranged in order. This process is called **collating**. The copies can be collated by hand or by machine. Some desktop publishing software has an optional print command that will produce collated copies. When the collate command is selected, one copy of all of the pages is printed before the second copy starts. Printing collated copies takes longer, because the information for each page must be sent to the printer each time for each copy.

- When bound publications are printed on a large press, several pages are printed together on a large sheet of paper and the paper is folded to page size. The folded printed sheet is called a **signature**. The number of pages in a signature is always a multiple of four. Book signatures most often contain 32 pages. The signatures are glued or stitched together at the spine. You can see the separate signatures in a book if you look at the end of the spine.

AT THE EDITOR'S DESK

Leslie tells you that he is pleased with how much you have learned about editing in the past few weeks. If you use everything that you have learned when you edit your own work, you will get a reputation for being a good writer. Here are a few suggestions to help you continue to improve your writing and editing skills.

1. Expand your vocabulary! The larger your vocabulary, the more effective your editing and writing will be. When you hear or see a word that you do not know, look it up in the dictionary. Make it a point to use the word in sentences until it becomes familiar to you—and the word will be yours forever.

2. When you are given a new editing assignment, read the entire text through at least once before you make any changes. Try to develop a good understanding of what the author is trying to tell the audience.
3. Edit first to make any needed changes in sentence structure, including grammar errors or organization. Remember, your objective is to make the author's message understandable to the audience.
4. Edit a second time for spelling and punctuation errors.
5. Read the text one more time to check for anything you may have missed.
6. People develop their own writing style. Keep in mind that a good editor strengthens the writing and corrects errors. That is, a good editor makes essential changes only, and does this without changing an author's style.

Here are two more proofreaders' marks for you to learn.

Proofreaders' Marks

⊙ ⊙ Circle periods and commas inserted in text to make them visible to the typist⊙

─── *ital.* This mark *ital.* means "set in italics."

| Name | Date | Period |

YOU, THE EDITOR!

Leslie tells you that after you finish two more assignments, you will be ready to work on your own. When you finish the work, write the date in the "Date Completed" column of your Work Assignment Log.

PART 1 HOW TO PRODUCE A NEWSLETTER

Instructions: Here is information that Andy has put together for people and organizations to use when they want to produce a newsletter. Leslie thinks it would be easier to understand if it were changed to a list of numbered points.

Example:

1. **About Newsletters.** Newsletters can be used to provide regular, specialized information to selected, limited audiences.

Review Andy's information to change it to numbered items. When you have completed your list of numbered items, key the information and add the list to your publishing handbook. Be creative! Some of the items will need to be completely rewritten to communicate effectively. Some may have more than one sentence. The sequence or order of some may need to be changed. Several sentences can be deleted. If you wish, you can make a brief, introductory paragraph from the material in the first paragraph. You will probably have about ten items.

GUIDELINES FOR PRODUCING A NEWSLETTER

Newsletters can provide regular, specialized information to selected, limited audiences. Most newsletters are from two to eight pages in length and are printed on 8 1/2 by 11-inch pages. Before deciding to produce a newsletter, you need to ask yourself, "What results do I want from this

---

Continued

newsletter?" The results expected are the objectives for your newsletter. The results should be stated in specific terms that everyone who is involved with the newsletter can understand.

Newsletters are most effective when written for people who have a common interest. The articles in the newsletter should stay within a narrow field of interest. That way the newsletter will continue to appeal to its audience. An effective newsletter is one that gives readers information they can use. Readers like inside information. If they think they are getting it from your newsletter, they will be faithful readers.

Your newsletters should communicate as effectively as the sentences, paragraphs, and articles contained in other publications.

Your newsletter must specialize. If you have more than one audience, consider writing more than one newsletter. Your audience should be so clearly defined that it can be described in one sentence. For example: The audience for our newsletter is made up of members of the Future Business Leaders of America Club.

Continued

Readers should be able to read the entire newsletter in just a few minutes. It will not hold their interest if it takes longer than that. Short, frequent newsletters work better than long ones that arrive less often.

How long it takes you to produce your newsletter depends on how quickly you write and how much help you have. After you have published the first issue, use the recorded time length for each phase of production--writing, desktop-publishing, producing copies--to establish a production schedule for future editions.

An effective newsletter name is one that sounds accurate and lively. Some newsletters use subtitles to make the purpose of the document more clear.

PART 2   EDITING AN ARTICLE

Instructions: Here is another article that has been brought in by a customer. The paragraphs need to be reorganized so the material flows more logically and is not redundant. Also, there are spelling and punctuation errors to correct. Please mark the editing changes on the copy so it can be rekeyed by someone else at a later date.

HOW TO IMPROVE YOUR MEMORY

Have you ever wondered why you can remember the plot of a book or movie you enjoyed but can't remember a social

Continued

studies reading assignment for 24 hours? That's because interest is one of the key principles of memory retention. If you are intensely interested in something, you don't have any problem remembering.

Many students have not had enough experience with living to understand what they will be able to do with things like multiplication tables and algebra. Often they learn in order to please parents or teachers or so that they can complete one class and move on to another. The important missing ingredient is interest. Students who are interested in math have an easier time memorizing their multiplication tables.

In order to understand memory, we need to understand why we forget. Sometimes we think we have forgotten something when the fact of the matter is we nmever learned it very well to start with. Incomplete learning is usually the result of a lack of interest or attention. Sometimes we forget deliberately. In order to concentrate, we fogret everything that is irrelevant to the purpose of the moment. We could not concentrate at all if we were unable to forget everything else for a short while.

We also forget things that make us ynhappy and we sometimes forget the names of people we don't like.

Continued

It is easier to remember things we understand completely. In fact, complete underatanding is necessary for good recall. We must also hav e the intention to remember. If you don't intend to remember something when you start learning, you will not be able to recall it.

A good tool to use in order to remember something is association. For instance, my friend's birthday is January 22. I could never remember this until I "associated" it with my own birthday on February 23. Now, I can remember his birthday because I remind myself it is one day and one month before my own.

Another way to help yourself remember is to organize things so that they are easy to understand or to work with. Things that are in a logical order are easier to remember. There are all kinds of helpful techniques to use to help you remember things. The key, however, is interest. Where you can generate interest, you will be able to remember successfully.

Name _____ Date _____ Period _____

EXPLORING DESKTOP PUBLISHING

DTP ACTIVITY 10A   PREPARING THE TABLE OF CONTENTS

Instructions: Organize the materials you have saved for your publishing handbook, and prepare a table of contents. Desktop-publish the table of contents.

1. Divide the pages into sections. You can organize them by chapter, by topic, or by other logical categories. Number the sections you decide to use. Consider using Roman numerals (I, II, III, etc.) for the section numbers.
2. Number the pages. Number the pages in each section starting with page 1. With this scheme, you can always add pages to a section. The page numbers or folios for each section will read I-1, I-2, I-3, etc.; II-1, II-2, II-3, etc.; III-1, III-2, III-3, etc. Place the folio in the same place on each page. For example, center the numbers at the top or bottom of each page or place them in the outside corner at the top or bottom. You can write the numbers neatly by hand or use a typewriter for a more professional look.
3. Originate the table of contents. With word processing or desktop publishing software, enter the section titles and titles of each page. Indent the page titles or set the section titles in a larger or bold type. Use a right tab to place the page numbers at the right margin. If possible, use dot leaders before the page numbers.
4. Print a proof copy of the table of contents. Proofread it carefully. Check to be sure you have entered the correct page numbers. Revise the table of contents file if necessary and print a final copy for your publishing handbook.

DTP ACTIVITY 10B   CREATING THE COVER AND TITLE PAGE

Instructions: Design a cover page. Use this design as the basis for a title page design. Desktop-publish both pages. Follow these steps:

1. Make several thumbnail sketches for a cover design. Include the handbook title, your name, and a graphic. Plan to use the Omega logo or a graphic of your own.
2. Select one of your sketches and develop a comprehensive layout for it.
3. Design the title page. Often the title page is a simplified version of the cover design. For example, you might use the same layout, but set the title in smaller type and make the graphic smaller. Include the title, your name, the name and location of your school, and the date of publication.

4. Desktop-publish the cover and title page. Consider printing the cover on colored **cover stock**, a heavy-weight paper made for covers, or photocopy it on colored cover stock.

DTP ACTIVITY 10C   COMPLETING THE PUBLISHING HANDBOOK

Instructions: To complete the publishing handbook, assemble the pages as follows:

1. Use a three-hole punch on the cover and on all of the pages.
2. You might want to make divider pages for the sections of the handbook. If the pages have tabs, label them with the section identification.
3. Collate the pages and insert them in the binder. Place the table of contents after the title page. Then arrange each section according to your plan.

Name _____ Date _____ Period _____

VOCABULARY REVIEW

vo·cab·u·lary

The following terms are used in Chapter 10 and are defined in the Glossary. Match the definitions to the terms by placing the letter of the correct definition in the space provided. Review Chapter 10 or the Glossary for any terms you do not remember. Not all definitions will be used.

Term	Definition
____ 1. front matter	A. the page number
____ 2. dot leaders	B. to punch paper
____ 3. folio	C. the binding used on this book
____ 4. spine	D. stapled together through the fold
____ 5. cover stock	E. to arrange pages in order
____ 6. perfect binding	F. a row of periods
____ 7. saddle stitching	G. appendices
____ 8. drill	H. title page and preface
____ 9. collate	I. heavy weight paper
____ 10. signature	J. the back edge of a book
	K. a group of pages printed on the same sheet

TREASURE HUNT

The final step in publishing a document such as the publishing handbook you have been working on is to collate and bind the pages. While you will use a loose leaf binder for the Omega handbook, you will want to consider other alternatives for binding future projects. How many examples of different bindings can you find?

Visit a local copy shop or print shop and find out what kinds of bindings are available. What are the pros and cons of each type? What is the cost of binding with each process? How long does it take? What steps are involved? Is there any special preparation that should be done, such as leaving extra space on the binding edge or splicing the original pages together if they will be printed on one sheet? If possible, obtain samples of bindings to share with the class.

WORK ASSIGNMENT LOG

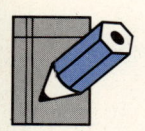

Fill in the "Date Assigned" and "Date Due" columns for each assignment that your teacher makes. When you complete an assignment, enter the date in the "Date Completed" column.

Chapter 10 Work Assignments	Date Assigned	Date Due	Date Completed
Software Check			
You, the Editor! Part 1			
You, the Editor! Part 2			
DTP Activity 10A			
DTP Activity 10B			
DTP Activity 10C			
Vocabulary Review			
Treasure Hunt			

Turn in Chapter 10 assignments after you have completed all of them, or follow your teacher's instructions. When these assignments are returned to you, put them in your publishing handbook.

APPENDIX A

PROOFREADERS' MARKS

Mark	Description	Example	Result
ℰ	Delete a character, word, phrase, or line	his ~~own~~ opinion is	his opinion is
∧	Insert	desk∧publishing (top)	desktop publishing
⌒	Close up a space	Omega Desk⌒top, Inc.	Omega Desktop, Inc.
#	Insert space	decision#making	decision making
∽	Transpose characters or words	to ⌜strongly⌝⌜state⌝	to state strongly
bf or 〜	Boldface	Boldface or Boldface	**Boldface**
stet ----	An editor's word meaning "Let it stand the way it was before I changed it."	~~high school~~ education stet	high school education
/lc	Lowercase	Use these marks (lc)	use these marks
≡ or ⓒap	Capitalize	use these marks or cap. use these marks	Use these marks

195

Mark	Description	Example	Result
⃝ sp	Spell out	⃝DTP sp.	desktop publishing
___	Underline	Koyama's Tips	Koyama's Tips
¶	Begin paragraph	Edit text to make it more specific.¶ Use selected marks.	Edit text to make it more specific. Use selected marks.
⊐	Move right	Start the computer ⊐and load the software.	Start the computer and load the software.
⊏	Move left	⊏Use selected marks in editing copy.	Use selected marks in editing copy.

‖	Align type; set flush	‖Align
		  type;
		    set flush
			Align
			type;
			set flush

⊓	Move up	move text ⊓up⌐	move text up
⊔	Move down	⌐move⌐ down	move down
=	Hyphen	Add a hyphen to Mexican⌃American =	Add a hyphen to Mexican-American
⊙ ⊙ ⊙ ⊙ ⊙	Insert a period, comma, apostrophe, question mark, colon, quotation marks, etc.	Punctuation is important⊙	Punctuation is important.
___ ital.	Set in italics	Type styles add interest to text. ital.	*Type styles* add interest to text.

CLICHÉS

Cliché is the French word for *stereotype*. A cliché is an expression that has been used over and over for many years until it loses its force. A good editor must be aware of the proper use for clichés. Sometimes it is better to use a cliché that saves a reader's time because of the message it conveys than to try to think of something new. The clichés to avoid are those that can be omitted or replaced with a more precise expression. Clichés are sometimes wordy as well as worn out. A few of these expressions also appear in the **Making Text More Concise by Eliminating Unnecessary Words and Phrases** and the **Redundant Phrases** lists included in this appendix.

1. accidents will happen
2. as old as the hills
3. fish or cut bait
4. poor as a church mouse
5. last but not least
6. the bottom line
7. leaps and bounds
8. enclosed please find
9. we would like to take this opportunity to
10. at one fell swoop
11. as luck would have it
12. as the crow flies
13. busy as a bee
14. far be it from me
15. fate worse than death
16. few and far between
17. food for thought
18. add insult to injury
19. no sooner said than done
20. exception that proves the rule
21. if the shoe fits
22. due consideration
23. dig in one's heels
24. dog in the manger
25. in no uncertain terms
26. hope springs eternal
27. green with envy
28. give the green light
29. generous to a fault
30. needs no introduction
31. no sooner said than done
32. nipped in the bud
33. never a dull moment
34. more than meets the eye
35. line of least resistance
36. leave well enough alone
37. labor of love
38. it goes without saying
39. dead as a doornail
40. cut a long story short
41. clear as mud
42. calm before the storm
43. burning the midnight oil
44. one and the same
45. other things being equal
46. own worst enemy
47. pros and cons
48. red-letter day
49. ripe old age
50. sadder but wiser
51. second to none
52. select few
53. vanish into thin air
54. viable alternative
55. massage the data
56. view with alarm
57. take the bull by the horns
58. this day and age
59. thank you in advance
60. leaves no stone unturned

REDUNDANT PHRASES

Redundant means unnecessarily repetitious. By eliminating the unnecessary (redundant) words from the following phrases, you can communicate more effectively and concisely.

Replace This:	With This:
1. delete out	delete
2. big in size	big, large
3. filled to capacity	full
4. blue in color	blue
5. classified into groups	classified
6. consensus of opinion	consensus
7. few in number	few
8. 4:00 p.m. in the afternoon	4:00 p.m.
9. strangled to death	strangled
10. appear to be	appear
11. as to whether	whether
12. last of all	last
13. skirt around	skirt
14. continue on	continue
15. lift up	lift
16. follow after	follow
17. hurry up	hurry
18. at some time to come	at some time
19. never at any time	never
20. graceful in appearance	graceful
21. they are both alike	they are alike
22. commute to and from	commute
23. eliminate altogether	eliminate
24. gather up	gather
25. connected together	connected
26. pair of twins	twins
27. one and the same	the same
28. and so as a result	and so, as a result *(use either expression)*
29. on the occasion when	when
30. each and every	each

FREQUENTLY MISSPELLED BUSINESS WORDS

absence
accommodate
achievement
acquisition
advisory
analysis
appreciate
appropriate
arrangement
assessment
benefit
brochure
calendar
capabilities
capacity
category
commitment
congratulations
consistent
consultant
continuous
contractor
convenience
development
eligible
expenditure
extension
extremely
financial
guarantee

individual
judgment
library
maintenance
management
minimum
opportunity
participate
particular
permanent
personnel
presenter
previous
probably
professional
questionnaire
receipt
receive
recommendation
referred
requirement
schedule
scientific
seminar
significant
substantial
supervisor
technical
techniques
thorough

MAKING TEXT MORE CONCISE BY ELIMINATING UNNECESSARY WORDS AND PHRASES

The following is a list of words and phrases that can be replaced with shorter words and phrases:

Replace This:	**With This:**
1. so that	so, to
2. despite the fact that	although, even though
3. seldom ever	seldom
4. terminate	end
5. in a timely manner	on time
6. subsequent to	after
7. in the vicinity of	near
8. inside of	within
9. a small number of	a few
10. on account of	because
11. as per our conversation	as we discussed
12. to give you a call	to call you
13. thanks in advance	thanks
14. enclosed please find	enclosed is
15. a large percentage of	many
16. at an early date	soon
17. during the time that	when, while
18. give assistance to	help
19. ahead of schedule	early
20. had occasion to be	was
21. in advance of	before
22. in this day and age	today
23. suburban area	suburb
24. take into consideration	consider
25. was of the opinion that	believed, thought
26. was witness to	saw
27. by the name of	named
28. call a halt to	stop
29. true facts	facts
30. great big	large, big

PUNCTUATION GUIDELINES

1. **Punctuation marks used to end sentences:**

   . *period*

   Marks the end of a sentence that makes a statement (declarative)
   (The bus is late.)

   ? *question mark*

   Marks the end of a sentence that asks a question (interrogative)
   (Will the bus ever come?)

   ! *exclamation point*

   Marks the end of a sentence that displays excitement, anger, joy or other strong feelings (exclamatory)
   (Here comes the bus!)

   Marks the end of a command (imperative)
   (Hurry—get on the bus!)

2. **Punctuation marks used in the body of a sentence:**

   , *comma*

   Separates sentence elements, for example:

   Two independent clauses joined by a coordinating conjunction
   (The lottery has brought wealth to many people, but it has not helped me at all.)

   Words, phrases, or clauses in a series
   (The children were told to pack a sleeping bag, a change of clothes, a towel and washcloth, and enough food for three days.)

   Separates two adjectives when each one can modify the noun
   (The girl had long, black hair.)

   Sets off a phrase in any part of the sentence—beginning, middle, or end
   (When I feel like dancing, I ask Jenny to go out with me. The wedding, originally scheduled for March 3, will take place on May 15. Perhaps we waste our time trying to get people to save their money, spending being the rule of the day.)

   Sets off the year from the month and the day
   (July 12, 1989)

   Separates parts of geographical names
   (Los Angeles, California)

   Indicates a word left out
   (James's coat was brown; Judy's, red.)

Distinguishes between a speaker and what he or she says
(Molly said, "Let's go on a picnic tomorrow.")

; *semicolon*

Separates clauses and phrases more definitely than a comma, but not as definitely as a period. For example:

Separates two or more independent clauses with or without conjunctive adverbs. Examples of conjunctive adverbs are *however, likewise, nevertheless, therefore, moreover, then, still,* and *yet.*
(The weather is very warm; however, I still think we should be prepared for rain. My regular flight is always on time; occasionally I miss it.)

: *colon*

Signals that a statement or list will follow. For example:

Introduces a series
(Robert has letters in three different sports: track, swimming, and water polo.)

Stresses a word, phrase, or clause that follows
(He has a malady that afflicts all of us sooner or later: spring fever.)

Introduces a quotation
(Robert Browning said: "The common problem, yours, mine, everyone's, is—not to fancy what were fair in life provided it could be—but, finding first what may be, then finding how to make it fair up to our means.")

Separates clauses when the second explains the first
(He needed the admiration of friends: admiration makes self-esteem blossom.)

Follows the salutation in a letter
(Dear Mrs. Jones:)

Separates parts of titles
(Omega Desktop, Inc.: A Desktop Publishing Simulation)

— *dash*

Has the force of a strong comma

Use the dash to mark a sudden or sharp turn in thought or sentence structure or an afterthought tacked on to the main thought
(Make the most of each day—today is the first day of the rest of your life.)

( ) *parentheses*

Enclose or set off supplementary or explanatory material not as important to the sentence as that set off by a comma or dash
(A period marks the end of a sentence (declarative) that makes a statement.)

Appendix A

" " *quotation marks*

Use quotation marks to enclose the actual words used by a writer or speaker, slang expressions or technical terms, and titles of poems or stories appearing in a larger work
(John said, "It's about time we leave for the game." His party is the only "game" in town. Her article, "The Time for Peace is Now," appeared in the paper last week.)

- *hyphen*

The hyphen joins two or more words used as a single adjective when they come before their noun
(a never-to-be-forgotten day)

STATE ABBREVIATIONS

AL	Alabama		MT	Montana
AK	Alaska		NE	Nebraska
AZ	Arizona		NV	Nevada
AR	Arkansas		NH	New Hampshire
CA	California		NJ	New Jersey
CO	Colorado		NM	New Mexico
CT	Connecticut		NY	New York
DE	Delaware		NC	North Carolina
FL	Florida		ND	North Dakota
GA	Georgia		OH	Ohio
HI	Hawaii		OK	Oklahoma
ID	Idaho		OR	Oregon
IL	Illinois		PA	Pennsylvania
IN	Indiana		RI	Rhode Island
IA	Iowa		SC	South Carolina
KS	Kansas		SD	South Dakota
KY	Kentucky		TN	Tennessee
LA	Louisiana		TX	Texas
ME	Maine		UT	Utah
MD	Maryland		VT	Vermont
MA	Massachusetts		VA	Virginia
MI	Michigan		WA	Washington
MN	Minnesota		WV	West Virginia
MS	Mississippi		WI	Wisconsin
MO	Missouri		WY	Wyoming

APPENDIX B

Appendix B 213

Chapter 2 Clip Art

PHONEPIC

Chapter 3 Clip Art

The Omega letterhead appears on the next right-hand page; it does not appear on the template disks.

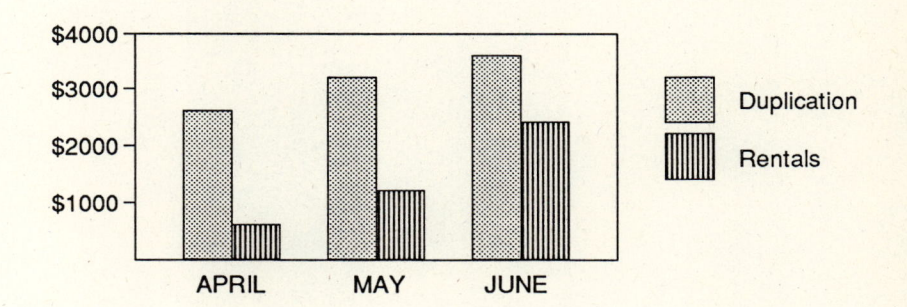

CHART3MO

VACATION    MEDICAL 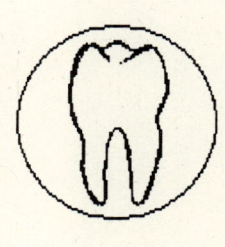   DENTAL    SICK 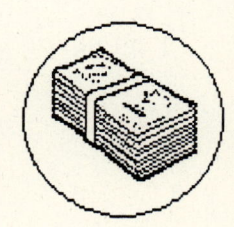   PROFITS

Ω OMEGA DESKTOP, INC.

3245 Custer Street
Santa Rosa, CA 98453

(787) 572-7778

Appendix B 217

Chapter 4 Clip Art

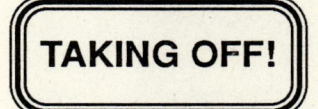

TAKING OFF!

TAKING OFF!

TAKING OFF!

TAKING OFF!

LABELS

The following items do not appear on the template disk:

WINGS

WINGS

Wings for Rent
453 Airport Road
Santa Rosa, CA 95401

Appendix B 219

Chapter 6 Clip Art

STEVENS

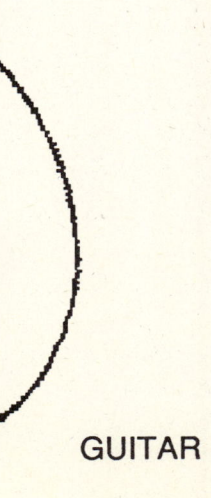

GUITAR

Appendix B 221

Chapter 7 Clip Art

RACER

Appendix B 223

Chapter 8 Clip Art

DTP1

DTP2

Appendix B 225

Chapter 9 Clip Art

The Omega DTP Job Order Forms appear on the next right-hand page; they do not appear on the template disks.

MG

LAMPPOST

BELL (8)

Omega DTP Job Order

Client: _____
Today's date: _____
Date due: _____
Description: _____
_____
_____
_____
_____
_____
_____

Files: _____
_____
_____

Omega DTP Job Order

Client: _____
Today's date: _____
Date due: _____
Description: _____
_____
_____
_____
_____
_____
_____

Files: _____
_____
_____

Omega DTP Job Order

Client: _____
Today's date: _____
Date due: _____
Description: _____
_____
_____
_____
_____
_____
_____

Files: _____
_____
_____

Omega DTP Job Order

Client: _____
Today's date: _____
Date due: _____
Description: _____
_____
_____
_____
_____
_____
_____

Files: _____
_____
_____

Appendix B 229

Chapter 10 Clip Art

Ω OMEGA
DESKTOP, INC.

OMEGLOGO

GLOSSARY

A

asymmetrical layout The layout is different on each half of the page.

B

back-to-back pages Two pages printed so that the second page is on the back of the first page. The first page is a right-hand page and the second page, a left-hand page.

bit-mapped graphics Computer drawings made by defining each tiny dot of light, called a *pixel*, that makes up the computer screen.

bleed Printing that extends to the edge of the paper.

bold A style in a given typeface that is heavier in weight than the regular style.

bold italic A style in a given typeface that is slanted and heavier in weight.

bullet list A listing of items or a series of short paragraphs, each of which is set off with a special character, such as a dot or checked box.

C

camera-ready copy Original work used as a master for reproducing copies. Also called *mechanical*.

centered Headings or lines of type that appear in the middle of a column or page.

cliché An expression that has been used over and over until it sounds lifeless and dull.

clicking Pressing a button on top of the mouse.

clip art Ready-made illustrations found in books or on disk. Such art can be used unchanged or modified to illustrate desktop publications.

collating Arranging in order.

color separation Process by which a different original is prepared for printing each different color of a publication.

comb binding A style of binding that uses a curled plastic strip to hold the pages of a publication together.

comp A detailed sample layout that closely resembles the final product. Short for *comprehensive*.

comprehensive See *comp*.

concise Expressed in a few words.

cover stock Heavy-weight paper that is made for publication covers.

crop To trim an illustration.

cursor A line or icon on the screen that shows where the next keyboard or clicking action will take place. The mouse cursor moves with the mouse and can have many shapes. The text cursor moves with the keys and is usually a blinking line or box.

cut To delete or remove a selected block of text or a graphic. The selection that is cut is stored in memory.

cut-and-paste To create an original by assembling cutout pieces of existing text and graphics on a page.

D

dangling modifier A modifier that does not clearly relate to another word.

default margins Preset margins that are part of the software features.

deselect To cancel or turn off a selection.

dialog box A boxed message from the program that asks for additional information.

display type Very large type used as a graphic element in page design.

dot leaders A row of periods or other symbols in the blank space between an item and a number, such as the title of a chapter and the page number in a table of contents.

double spread A layout of two facing pages designed to be viewed together.

draw programs Programs that make files that contain instructions for drawing objects. Draw programs create object-oriented graphics.

drill To make holes similar to those made by a three-hole punch. A special machine can make holes through more than 2,000 pages at one time.

drop cap A large initial capital that is lowered so that its top is even with the top of the other smaller letters on the first line of the text.

E

emphasize To call attention to a specific item or point.

enlarge To make larger or increase in size.

F

facing pages Two pages printed so that they are side-by-side. The first page is a left-hand page and the second page, a right-hand page.

file conversion software Software that can convert or change files so that they can be used by other software.

fill patterns Designs or patterns, such as dots, dashes, lines, basket weave, and brick, that are used to fill an enclosed area or background.

flush right The ends of the lines are even at the right margin. Also called *right justified*.

folio Page numbers that appear on every page of a document.

font The information required to display or print a typeface in a particular style and size. *Helvetica italic 10 point* is a font. (See also printer font and screen font.)

footer A line of information that is printed at the bottom of each page.

formatting codes Special codes in word processing files that tell the screen and printer how to display and print the text.

freehand Drawing by hand without using mechanical aids.

freehand tool A computer graphic tool used to draw free-form shapes that are not geometric.

front matter The title page, preface, table of contents, and other pages that appear before the first section or chapter of a publication.

G

gray-mapped files Graphic files that show tones or shades of gray as well as black and white.

grid A pattern of vertical and horizontal guidelines showing page margins, columns, etc., that are used to locate elements on a page.

guidelines Lines used to align or place text and graphic elements. Guidelines do not print.

gutter The space between columns.

H

header A line of information that is printed at the top of each page.

hyphenation Division of words at the ends of lines using the hyphen.

I

icons Small pictures representing choices such as pointing, entering text, drawing boxes, etc.

importing files To read a file from disk and bring it into a DTP program. The contents of the imported file can then be placed on the page.

insertion point The place in the text where keystrokes will appear; or, the location of the text cursor.

italic A type style with slanting letters.

J

justified Lines of type that are spread so that both the left and the right margins are even.

K

kern To adjust the amount of space between a pair of letters.

L

landscape A horizontal page orientation, wider than it is tall.

large initial cap The first letter that is set in larger type than the other letters in a section of text.

leading Spacing between lines of type, measured in points. The term *leading* comes from the thin strips of lead typesetters insert between lines of metal type.

letterspacing The amount of spacing between the letters within a word.

light-blue pencil A tool used to draw guidelines and make notes on originals. The light-blue lines will not show when a copy is made.

light table A glass-covered table or box that contains bright lights. A light table is used for stripping.

M

makeover A redesigned format for a publication planned to improve its appearance.

master page(s) The page grid(s) used for all right-hand (and left-hand) pages in a publication. A master page can also include the page number location, headers and footers, and graphic elements such as rules.

mechanical See *camera-ready*.

menu bar The bar at the top of the screen where menu titles appear.

mirror To reverse the margin measurements for facing pages so the narrow margin appears on the opposite side on left-hand and right-hand pages.

misplaced modifiers Modifiers that are in the wrong place and appear to modify something else. See *modifier*.

modifier A word or phrase that adds to the meaning of other sentence elements by describing them.

monospaced The amount of space used for all characters is the same, regardless of the width of each character. For example, the same space is taken up for an *M* as for an *I*.

mouse A hand-held device for moving the mouse pointer on the screen.

mouse pad A special mat designed to make the mouse ball roll easily.

mouse pointer The arrow-shaped cursor that moves on the screen when the mouse is moved.

N

normal Specifies the vertical, not bold type style (also called *roman*).

O

object-oriented graphics Computer drawings made by connecting points on the screen to draw lines and shapes.

orientation The layout of the page as a vertical (portrait/tall) or horizontal (landscape/wide) page (also called *page orientation*).

original The page from which copies are made.

P

page area On a computer screen, the rectangle representing the paper on which text and graphics are arranged.

page grid The layout of margins and columns for a page.

page orientation See *orientation*.

paint programs Programs that make bit-mapped graphics.

panels Printed sections separated by space where the paper will be folded.

parallelism Sentence elements that closely correspond to each other. Parallel elements separated by coordinate conjunctions (*and*, *but*, *or*) must be parallel in form: A noun must parallel a noun, etc.

paste To insert a selected block of text or a graphic that has been cut or copied.

pasteup The process of combining text and graphic elements manually by fastening them to a sheet of paper.

perfect binding A binding in which the cover is wrapped around the spine and the pages are glued to the cover at the spine.

pica A unit of measurement traditionally used to measure type and typeset documents. There are six picas in an inch.

pick-up A chunk of dried rubber cement used to remove excess cement from an original.

pixel A picture element; one of the tiny dots of light that makes up the image on the computer screen.

place To import a text or graphic file and position it on the page.

placeholder An empty box that shows where a graphic or text block will go.

plastic template A thin plastic sheet with cutout shapes, such as circles, ellipses, special symbols, etc., that is used in manual drawing to reproduce these shapes on paper.

point One-twelfth of a pica. There are 72 points in an inch.

portrait A vertical page orientation, taller than it is wide.

PostScript A page description language that tells a compatible printer how to print a page, including the font to use, the size of the type, the text to be printed, the position of all elements on the page, and any other necessary instructions.

preface An introduction that tells the purpose of a publication and describes its features.

printer font Information stored on disk, tape, or ROM chips that tells the printer how to produce a particular typeface, style, and size. On a PostScript printer, one font produces all sizes of a particular typeface and style.

proof A copy printed for checking a layout for changes needed before printing the final copy.

proofreaders' marks Special notes that editors use to show how copy should be changed.

proofreading Checking text for grammar and punctuation errors, misspelled words, incorrect names or numbers, and missing words or sentences.

proportionally spaced   The amount of space taken up by each character varies, depending upon the width of each character. For example, more space is allotted for an *M* than for an *I*.

pull-down menu   A list of commands that appears when you point to the menu title.

pull quote   The display of a short paragraph or sentence that makes a point in the text by setting it in large, bold type. Pull quotes are usually separated from the text by a rule above and below.

R

redundancy   Unnecessary repetition in a phrase, such as *follow after*.

reverse   Changing the letters so they appear white on black instead of black on white.

right justified   See *flush right*.

roman   Specifies a vertical (as opposed to italic) type style or a typeface that has line strokes of varying thickness (also called *normal*).

rule   A vertical or horizontal line used to organize a page, such as a vertical line between columns, or horizontal lines separating blocks of type.

rulers   Scales displayed at the edges of the working screen to help guide placement and sizing of text and graphics.

runaround   Type that is set to fit around a graphic.

S

saddle stitch binding   A wire binding that resembles staples. The wire used for saddle stitch binding is usually contained on large spools, similar to oversized spools of string. The length of the stitch and the number of stitches can therefore be adjusted for each specific document.

sans serif   Without serifs, or finishing strokes, on the ends of letter strokes. A sans serif typeface is a face without serifs.

scanner   A machine that translates a drawing or photo into data the computer can use to recreate the image on the screen and in printed form. Some scanners can also read pages of text and translate them into text files for word processing or DTP programs.

screen capture software   Program that stores a bit-mapped picture or screen shot of the information appearing on a computer screen.

screen font   A software file that displays characters in a particular typeface, style, and size on the computer screen.

scroll bars Parts of the program screen display used to move a page or list of options in its window in order to expose items not showing.

serif The finishing strokes on the ends of a letter stroke. A typeface with serifs is called a *serif face*.

shadow box A rectangle in a document that appears to have a shadow behind it. This can be achieved when two adjacent sides are drawn with thicker lines than the two opposite sides.

sidebar A display of text that provides additional information related to the main body of an article.

side head A heading for a section that appears to the left of the section and begins on the same line as the beginning of the section.

signature Several pages of a publication that are originally printed on a single large sheet that is then folded and cut together as a group of pages.

skew To distort.

snap-to grid A grid pattern that can be set to align type and graphics on the computer screen.

spine The inside edges of a publication where the pages are bound.

spiral binding A style of binding that uses a spiral curl of wire to hold the pages together.

stripping A manual technique for combining text and graphic elements into an original for photocopying or printing.

symmetrical layout The page layout is the same on each half of the page.

synonym A word that has the same meaning as another word.

T

template Master pages or page grids saved and used as a pattern for specific documents, such as newsletters, brochures, reports, etc.

thesaurus A reference used to find synonyms for words. Today a thesaurus might be in print or on a disk.

thumbnail sketches Small drawings that show roughly where blocks of text and graphics might be placed on a page.

title page A page that lists the title and other information about a publication.

tool box A group of boxed icons representing tools used with text or graphics in the DTP program.

transpose To change the sequence or order.

two-up Printing two copies on the same sheet of paper.

type alignments The various ways that type can be placed or aligned, such as justified and centered.

typeface A set of characters of the same design.

type family A group of typefaces based on the same design, such as Helvetica, Helvetica Narrow, and Helvetica Outline.

type style Variation of a typeface, such as normal, italic, and bold.

W

waxer Device used for spreading heated wax on a cutout for manual pasteup.

weak modifiers Modifiers that are vague, redundant, or dull.

window The frame through which the page is viewed.

WYSIWYG (What You See Is What You Get) Describes the ability of the DTP software to display the page on the screen exactly as it will look when printed.

INDEX

A

abbreviations, state, 209
agreement, grammatical, 101–102
align (proofreaders' mark), 145, 196
alignment, type, 151
appendices, 177
Arabic numbering, 176
asymmetrical, 115
    layout, 96–97

B

back-to-back, printing, 98
binding, 101, 177–178
    comb, 177
    and layout, 101
    loose-leaf binder, 178
    perfect, 177, 191
    saddle stitching, 177, 191
    spiral, 177
bit-mapped graphics, 119, 123, 143
bleed, 41, 53
boldface (proofreaders' mark), 42, 195
bold italic (type style), 76
bullet list, 97–98, 115

C

Cairo (special purpose font), 78
camera-ready copy, 155
cap
    drop, 138, 151
    large initial, 138
capitalize (proofreaders' mark), 82, 195
captions, type sizing for, 77
capture, screen software, 123, 135
centered, 151
    heads, 138–139
changing imported text, 41
cliché, 23–24, 33, 197
clicking, 5, 9, 15
clip art, 18, 33
close up (proofreaders' mark), 24, 195
codes, formatting, 23, 33
coding for table of contents and index, 181
collate, 181, 191
color separation, 143, 151
column, single, 138
column widths, preferred, 96
comb binding, 177
commands, entering with desktop publishing software, 9
commas and periods, insert (proofreaders' mark), 182, 196
comp, 154–155, 173
company logos, 54
completing publication process, 181
comprehensive
    See comp

concise text, 10, 15, 203
consistency in page design, 97–98
contents, table of, 176–177, 181
contrast, in page design, 97, 101
conversion, software for file, 123
copy, camera-ready, 155
copyright laws and typefaces, 81
Courier typeface, 77
cover stock, 190, 191
crop, 98, 115
cursor, 13
cut-and-paste, 56
cutouts, attaching to pasteup, 61

D

dangling modifiers, 102, 143–144
default margins, 19, 33
delete (proofreaders' mark), 10, 195
deselect, 9, 15
design
    and binding, 101
    contrasting elements on page, 97, 101
designers, typeface, 77–78
desktop publishing
    combining illustrations with text, 18–19
    commands, entering, 9
    importance of graphics and text, 4
    software, 9
    software features, 143, 159
    special effects, 143
dialog box, 9, 13–15
disk drives, 5–6
display type, 101, 115
dot leader, 177, 191
double spread, 98, 115
    and binding, 101
down, move text (proofreaders' mark), 161, 196
draw program, 119, 135
drill, 178, 191
drop cap, 138, 151
Dutch typeface, 81

E

editing, 9–10, 23–24, 41–42, 61–63, 82, 101–103, 123–125, 143–145, 160–161, 181–182
emphasis, in sentences, 124–125
    use of short sentences for, 160–161
emphasize, 160, 173
enlarge, 15
    with PostScript, 81
    window contents, 9
extensions, file, 23

F

facing pages, 98
features, desktop publishing software, 143, 159

file
    conversion software, 123, 135
    formats, 23
    graphic formats, 123
    gray-mapped, 123, 135
    large, 123
fill pattern, 118, 135
floppy disk drives, 5–6
flush, set (proofreaders' mark), 145, 196
flush right, 139
folio, 176–177, 191
font, 76, 81, 93
    printer, 81
    screen, 81
footer, 138, 151
footnotes, type sizing for, 77
formats, file, 23
    for graphics, 123
formatting codes, 23, 33
freehand, 135
freehand tool, 118
front matter, 177, 191

G

Geneva typeface, 81
graphic files
    formats, 123
    importing, 23, 118
graphic images, 123
graphic programs, 119
graphics, 118
    types of, 119
gray-mapped files, 123, 135
grid, 41, 53
    page, 96, 115
    pattern, 159
    snap-to, 159, 173
    thumbnail sketches and, 41
gutter, 90, 93

H

hard disk drive, 6, 9
head, side, 138, 151
header, 138
headlines
    centered, 138–139
    consistency in, 97–98
    sizing, 77
Helvetica Narrow typeface, 76
Helvetica Outline typeface, 76
Helvetica typeface, 76, 81
Helv typeface, 81
hyphenate (proofreaders' mark), 161, 196
hyphenation, 159–160, 173

I

icons, 9, 13, 15
illustrations, placing, 36–37

241

import, 33
imported text, 41
importing
    graphic files, 23, 118
    text and graphics, 23
    text files, 19, 23
index, 181
initial cap, large, 138
insert
    periods, commas, etc. (proofreaders' mark), 182, 196
    space (proofreaders' mark), 24, 195
    word, character, etc. (proofreaders' mark), 10, 195
insertion point, 37, 53
italic, 93
    type style, 76
italicize (proofreaders' mark), 182, 196

J

justified text, 138, 151
    and letterspacing, 159

K

kern, 159, 173
kerned pairs, 159

L

landscape (page orientation), 19, 33
large initial cap, 138
large type sizes, kerning, 159
layout
    asymmetrical, 96–97
    and binding, 101
    page, 36
    page considerations with, 101
    symmetrical, 96–97
    tools, 41, 56
    and thumbnail sketches, 96–97
    variety, 97
leading, 77, 93
left or right, move (proofreaders' mark), 125, 196
letters, kerned pairs of, 159
letterspacing, 159, 173
light-blue pencil, 56, 61
light table, 61, 73
logos, company, 54
loose sentences, 125
lowercase (proofreaders' mark), 63, 195

M

makeover, 155, 173
manual pasteup techniques, 61
margin, 36
    and binding, 101
    default, 19, 33
    and grids, 41
master pages, 96

measurements
    options with desktop publishing software, 41
    with type sizes, 77
mechanical, 173
    See also camera-ready copy
menu, 9
    pull-down, 9, 13, 15
menu bar, 13
mirroring, 115
    and layouts, 101
misplaced modifiers, 144
misspelled words, 42, 201
modifier, 102, 115, 143
    dangling, 102, 143
    misplaced, 144
    weak, 144
monospaced, 81, 93
Morison, Stanley, 77
mouse, 5, 15
    clicking, 5, 9
    and snap-to grid, 159
mouse pad, 5
mouse pointer, 13
move text
    down (proofreaders' mark), 161, 196
    left or right (proofreaders' mark), 125, 196
    up (proofreaders' mark), 145, 196

N

New Century Schoolbook typeface, 76–77
newsletters, guidelines for producing, 183–185
New York typeface, 81
normal type style, 76
numbering pages, 176–177

O

object-oriented graphics, 119
Optima typeface, 77
orientation, 33
    page, 19
original, 56, 73

P

page, title, 176
page area, 13
page design
    consistency within, 97–98
    contrast within, 97, 101
    templates, 101
page grid, 96, 115
page layout, 36
    considerations for, 101
page numbers, 181
pages, numbering, 176–177
page orientation, 19
    landscape, 13, 19
    portrait, 19, 33
paint program, 119, 135, 143

paint tools, 143
Palatino typeface, 76, 81
panels, 150
paragraph, 123–125
    set new (proofreaders' mark), 103, 196
parallelism in grammar, 102–103
pasteup, 56–57, 73
    contrasted with stripping, 61
    techniques, 61
perfect binding, 177, 191
periodic sentences, 125
period or comma, insert (proofreaders' mark), 182, 196
photographs, as gray-mapped files, 123
phrases, redundant, 199
pica, 41, 53
    and column width, 96
pick-up, rubber cement, 61, 73
pixel, 119, 123, 135
placeholder, 171, 173
placing illustrations, 36
planning worksheet for project, 170
plastic template, 56, 73
point, 41, 53
    and type sizes, 77
portrait page orientation, 19, 33
poster, 118
PostScript, 81, 93
preface, 177
    needless, 144
printer fonts, 81
printers, 143
printing, saving time with, 123
printing pages with graphics and text, 123
project planning worksheet, 170
proof, 37, 53
proofreaders' marks, 10, 15, 24, 42, 63, 82, 103, 125, 145, 161, 182, 195–196
proofreading, 24, 33
proportionally spaced typefaces, 81
publication, questions to ask when beginning, 154
publication process, completing, 181
publishing handbook, creating, 5
pull-down menu, 9, 13, 15
pull quote, 139, 151
punch, three-hole, 178
punctuation, 82
    guidelines for, 205–207

Q

questions to ask when beginning a publication, 154

R

reducing with PostScript, 81
redundancies, 41–42, 53
redundant phrases, 42, 199
reverse, 118, 135
right-justified, 139

Roman numerals, 177
roman type style, 77
rule, 96–98, 115
rulers, 13, 36, 53
runaround, 139, 151

S

saddle stitching, 177, 191
sans serif, 93
    typefaces, 76–77, 97
scanner, 57, 73
screen capture software, 123, 135
screen fonts, 81
scroll bars, 9, 13
sentences, emphasis in, 124–125
    types of, 125
sentence variation, 160–161
serif, 93
    typeface, 76–77, 97
set flush (proofreaders' mark), 145, 196
shaded boxes, 143
    lines, 143
shadow box, 118, 135
sidebar, 139, 143, 151
    tinting used with, 143
side heads, 138, 151
signature, 181, 191
skew, 157, 173
snap-to grid, 159, 173
software
    features in desktop publishing, 143
    file conversion, 123, 135
    screen capture, 123, 135
software manual, 6
space, insert (proofreaders' mark) 24, 195
special effects in desktop publishing, 143
spell out (proofreaders' mark), 82, 196
spine, 177, 191

spiral binding, 177
state abbreviations, 209
stet (proofreaders' mark), 63, 195
stripping, 61, 73
    contrasted with pasteup, 61
subheads, consistency of, 97–98
submenu, 9, 14
substitute typefaces, 81
Swiss typeface, 81
symmetrical layout, 96–97
synonym, 61, 73

T

table of contents, 176–177, 181
template, 101, 115
    for poster, 118
text
    and conciseness, 10
    justified, 138
    optimal size for reading, 77
text and graphics, importing, 23
text files, importing, 19, 23
thesaurus, 62, 73
three-hole punch, 178
thumbnail sketch, 36, 41, 53, 96
    and grid, 41
    and layouts, 96–97
Times Roman, 76, 77, 81
title bar, 13
title page, 176
tool box, 13
tools, layout, 41, 56
topic sentence, 123–125
transpose, 53
    (proofreaders' mark), 42, 195
two-up, 69
type, choosing, 78
type alignment, 139, 151
typeface, 76–78, 81, 93, 97
    copyright laws and, 81
    monospaced, 81, 93

    proportional, 81
    sans serif, 76–77
    serif, 76–77
substitute, 81
typeface designers, 77–78
type family, 76
type sizes, recommended column widths and, 96
    measuring, 77
type style, 76, 93

U

underline (proofreaders' mark), 103, 196
up, move text (proofreaders' mark), 145, 196

V

variation in sentences, 160–161
variety in page layouts, 97

W

waxer, 61, 73
weak modifiers, 144
white space, 97
window, 9, 15
wordiness, 62–63
    types of, 41
    See also cliché *and* redundancies
words, misspelled, 42, 201
words and phrases, needless, 203
working screen, 13
worksheet, project planning, 170
WYSIWYG, 23, 33

Z

Zapf, Hermann, 77
Zapf Chancery typeface, 77
Zapf Dingbats (special purpose font), 77–78